Praise for
The Light Within

"Liz L'Eclair's book, *The Light Within*, is insightful and captivating. She delves into the power of the subconscious mind and guides readers on a transformational journey toward healing. She dives deep into the concept of inner work and the exercises guide the reader into true power. A must read for all seekers."

Gina L. Santiago, Ammo Specialist, Sergeant First Class, United States Army Special Operations Command, FT Liberty, NC

"I was blown away at how much high-level content Dr. Liz was able to break down with great insight and background information. I enjoyed the personal stories on working these protocols into real life! I am taking the exercises to heart!"

Joy Richardson, Holistic Practitioner, Reiki Master, and Coach

"I'm so glad my friend Liz has put her wisdom to print. Her high IQ, strong intuition and emotional intelligence combined with an unusual breadth of experience: from taking on child soldiers of Uganda, to serving as a Special Forces Chaplain, to serving in the Middle East during the withdrawal of US troops from Afghanistan, to riding her Indian Scout motorcycle anywhere and everywhere makes for an approach to life and personal power that is like nothing else. Congrats Liz! You've done a great thing, and your readers will surely be blessed and expanded for spending time with *The Light Within*."

Sylvia Heins, Co-founder of Sädé Journeys, SadeJourneys.com

"And so here it is – a book that explains how our environment affects us and keeps us from our best selves. *The Light Within* contains numerous exercises and affirmations and I recommend the reader practice them. I have had great results with the concepts since Liz has also been my coach and friend. If you already have a mindfulness practice, check out Exercise #2. Turn your life into a movie and imagine being the person you need to be to attract what you desire. You will notice new opportunities showing up immediately. Exercise #5 helps us alter our mindset from negative to positive without freaking out. This book will guide you step by step on becoming the best you. Act! Enjoy!"

Luz E. Varela, Architectural Home Design and Artist

"Dr. L'Eclair lives and practices the principles in this book. I sensed immediately when I met her that she possessed knowledge that would help me be the best version of me. She has been teaching me the principles in this book since the day I met her and I am so grateful that they are now all written down for me to review daily. As I practice these principles, I have more joy and peace in my life, regardless of externals. As I read through each page I am thrilled with the possibilities. Greatness awaits. I hope you will join me on this journey."

LT David M. Ferguson, US Navy Chaplain

"Liz's wealth of personal experience as a US Army chaplain, pastor, shaman and coach has given her a vast storehouse of wisdom, knowledge, tips and tricks which she shares with her clients. Her personal positivity, integrity and self-discipline are inspirational. Just talking with Liz puts a new positive spin on a situation because of her kind, yet fearless, nature. I had a few rough patches and Liz used those experiences to show me how to work through them, learn from them and become stronger. I enthusiastically recommend Liz L'Eclair's book to anyone in transition, seeking to jumpstart their career or personal mission, or who simply wants to create a better and richer life."

Anne Kuespert, Massage Therapist and Cosmetologist Extraordinaire

"I'm a shamanic practitioner and Liz is my shaman! Her book is a powerful, knowledgeable, and talented work. Read it, it can help with anything spiritual, mental, physical, or relational. It also helps you remove any 'dark stuff' if you find you have it."

Jess – Mama Jaguar

"I read Liz's book – before, I could barely walk since I was in such pain, and my family in TN was driving me crazy. I imagined full health using techniques in the book. After a few weeks they helped with the pain first, and when I felt better, the energy work helped so much with how to manage my toxic family. I'm flying high now after absorbing all the help in her book!"

Aaron Villalobos, Cyber Security Specialist with the Department of Defense

"Dr. Liz L'Eclair's guidance in *The Light Within* helped to overcome my anxiety in truly exceptional ways. Her professional and empathetic approach with her techniques made the transformative journey incredibly meaningful. The speed at which I shifted from negative thoughts to motivational thinking highlighted Dr. Liz's mastery and tailored approach. Her deep understanding of psychological intricacies and insightful root-cause exploration set her apart. The impact of her interventions in the book extends beyond simple anxiety relief, providing enduring tools for daily resilience. For anyone seeking a compassionate and skilled guide through anxiety, *The Light Within* offers a shining beacon of expertise. My transformative experience with her book has left me immensely grateful for the positive changes she facilitated in my life."

LTC Irene Meddeb, 352 Combat Sustainment Support Commander, Macon, GA

"This is a great book for anyone who wants to overcome the inner obstacles that keep them from living a full and complete life of their dreams. By weaving her advice with neuroscience, practical steps, and recommended daily routines, Dr. L'Eclair offers excellent tools that anyone can use to enhance their life experiences. Our biggest challenges are those that we create in our own minds, and Liz has provided a wonderful way for people to rewire their own brains to realize their dreams."

Dr. Daniel Roberts, CSM for United States Army Reserve Command, Ft Liberty, NC; President and CEO, Moral Injury Support Network for Servicewomen, Inc.

"What is most powerful to me about the energic technology Liz offers with this book is that I don't need anyone else to do it. I don't need to be in a certain place or at a certain time, I don't need to pay more than the price of a book—I can create transformation and lasting ease and abundance as I am, now, here. It seems too good to be true—too easy. And yet, it works. As I continue to practice this energetic technology, I am finding that perhaps, as Liz posits repeatedly throughout this book, life IS meant to be 97% awesome and amazing, and only 3% unpleasant. I am coming to trust that ease, abundance, and joy are endlessly available to everyone. This is totally worth the work required, work that Liz clearly and colorfully lays out in this potent text."

Bekah Giacomantonio, CEO for Lunadesk, Embodied Mindfulness Teacher and Entrepreneur

"The author's strength lies in her unwavering commitment to help others instill a positive mindset. Through her insights, affirmations, and practical strategies, she helps you break free from a stuck mindset and embrace a life filled with hope, purpose, prosperity and the unending possibilities of positivity. I am forever thankful for her help and encouragement!"

Brenda Gugino, CEO Lakeshore Genii, Home Organizing Specialists

"I have known Liz for years, and she is the embodiment of everything in this book. I feel like a smarter, better person for it. I think you will, too."

William J. Gephart, PA, Retired Special Forces 18D NCO, Current Advanced Medical Instructor at the United States Army's Joint Special Operations Medical Training Center

THE LIGHT WITHIN

NAVIGATING THE WORLD OF
ENERGY AND CONSCIOUSNESS

Liz L'Eclair, Ph.D.

Copyright © 2024 Liz L'Eclair

All rights reserved. No part of this publication in print or in electronic format may be reproduced, stored in a retrieval system, or transmitted in any form or by any means, electronic, mechanical, photocopying, recording, or otherwise without the prior written permission of the publisher.

The scanning, uploading, and distribution of this book without permission is a theft of the author's intellectual property. Thank you for your support of the author's rights.

Editing, design, and distribution by Bublish
Published by L'Eclair Publishing

ISBN: 978-1-647047-93-1 (eBook)
ISBN: 978-1-647047-92-4 (paperback)
ISBN: 978-1-647047-95-5 (audiobook)

Dedication

Thank you to my gorgeous and brilliant children: Jake, Bekah, Lance, Kat, Veronica, Meena, and Grace. I also thank my soldiers, sailors, and marines; it was an honor to serve you; I am a better person because of all of you. My amazing and powerful friends have helped me through life's interesting roller-coaster turns, and I love all of you very much.

Why Should You Read This Book?

- What if you could remove perceived limitations such that you could live the life you truly want?
- What if you could craft thrilling and fulfilling life experiences?
- What if you could have health, abundance, love, personal power, work contentment, and fame?
- What if you were able to protect yourself from troublesome energies?
- What if you could access brilliant and creative energies and tap into the powerful minds of geniuses, living or dead?
- What if you were an intense magnet, attracting everything you desire?
- What if you could develop a beautiful high-mindedness and acculturation in which you know your own beauty and could attract people, wealth, and goods?
- What if you could have the skills to offer the world new creativity and healing?
- What if you employed your personality to remote sense, influence, and view places and situations?
- What if you healed your own soul and personality and those of your friends, family, and pets?

Contents

Introduction xvii
A Gentle Disclaimer xxi

Chapter 1: The Three Minds 1
   Superconscious Mind 1
   Conscious Mind 2
   Subconscious Mind 2
   Mental Diet 4
   Quantum Rewiring—Managing Trauma 5
   The bad guys 6
   The Systems 7
      Play It Smooth 9
      Play It Strange 9

Chapter 2: Baseline Work 11
   Exercise 1—Baseline Mirror Work 11
   Exercise 2—Your Part in the Movie 13
   Exercise 3—Daily Mirror Work 14
   Mindset Redux 16
   Exercise 4—Mindset Work 16
   Exercise 5—The Elimination List 17

Chapter 3: Beginning Energy Work 21
   Exercise 6—Your Magnetic Aura 21
   Exercise 7—Grounding and Running Energy 24
   Exercise 8 — Chakra Balancing 26

Chapter 4: Spiritual Protection 31
Exercise 8—Managing Awful People 32
Exercise 9—Protection—Defense 33
Exercise 10—Protection—Offense 35

Chapter 5: Charging Your Magnetic Biofield 37
Exercise 11—Powering Up Your Magnetic Field 37
Exercise 12—Move It into Your Aura 39

Chapter 6: Projecting Your Golden Aura 41
Mental Movies 41
Exercise 13—Write Down Your Desires 41
Exercise 14—Create Your Mental Movies 42
    Mental Movies for the Right Work 43
    Mental Movies for Finding Love 43
    Mental Movies for Health, Energy, and Long Life 43
    Mental Movies for Great Wealth 44

Chapter 7: Attract and Influence People 47
Exercise 15—Watch Your Tone 50
People Skills 50
Remote Sensing/Viewing/Influencing 52
Exercise 16—Remote Sensing, Viewing, and Influencing 53

Chapter 8: Improving Your Health 57
Fear 58

Chapter 9: Your Cosmic Committee 63
Exercise 17—Form Your Committee 64

Chapter 10: Cosmic Rhythms and Law of Time 67
Cosmic Rhythms 67
Exercise 18—Playing with Cosmic Rhythms 68
Exercise 19—Time Is Not Law—Another Way to Play with Rhythm and Timing 70

Chapter 11: A Really Big Goal 73
Exercise 20—Dream Big 74
Exercise 21—Self-Confidence 76

Chapter 12: What to Do When You're Freaking Out ... 77
Exercise 22—Create Your Self-Soothe List 78

Chapter 13: Some Great Affirmations 81
Bright and Positive 81
Ways to Use Affirmations 82
Don't Be Desperate 82
Time Lag 83
The Date Is Not Important 83
Be Present 83
Leave Room for Something Better 84
Using Key Words 84
Askformations 84
"I Am" Statements 84
Using Anthony Norvell's Key Word Program Method 85
Being Grateful 87
Some Great Affirmations 88

Chapter 14: My Daily Things 97
How to Begin 101

Introduction

You and everything on the earth are made up of energy, vibration, and light. There is some science that supports this. Quantum physics suggests that humans are 0.0000001 percent physical matter and 99.9999999 percent energy, vibration, and light.[1] Some have suggested that the actual atomic matter of every human on the planet could be condensed[2] to the size of one sugar cube.[3] This is ironic, since we are so concerned with our physical bodies and our five senses in this material reality, yet we are mostly energy.

Dr. Rupert Sheldrake performed experiments suggesting that dogs know exactly when their owners are on their way home from work. A significant number of dogs reacted excitedly at that very moment.[4] The astronaut Edward Mitchell performed successful telepathic experiments with Dr. Joseph Rhine while aboard Apollo 14. Dr. Rhine developed the Zener symbols: simple symbols on cards such as a square, a circle, and a cross. These were represented by

---

[1] Based on knowledge of the atom—for example: https://www.britannica.com/science/atom/Atomic-bonds.

[2] McTaggart, Lynn. *The Field: The Quest for the Secret Force of the Universe*, Harper Collins, 2002, pp. 5–10.

[3] Musings by Ali Sundermier: https://www.sciencealert.com/99-9999999-of-your-body-is-empty-space

[4] https://www.sheldrake.org/research/animal-powers/a-dog-that-seems-to-know-when-his-owner-is-coming-home-videotaped-experiments-and-observations

numbers, which Mitchell telepathically sent to Dr. Rhine. The results were significant, indicating a one in three thousand probability, which was the result of pure chance. This knowing—this communication—occurs because of the continual vibrations and fluctuations in the (alleged) vacuum of space or the field.

The field is in every part of space and is in continual contact with all of itself. Dr. Hal Puthoff, while a researcher at Stanford Research Institute, worked through some quantum calculations and developed, with other scientists before him, the concept of the zero-point field.[5] This is another way to describe the Heisenberg uncertainty principle, in which you can know the speed of a particle but not its momentum, and vice versa. It describes atomic particles popping in and out of the vacuum of space. Puthoff suggested that a particle is always a particle and does not shift into a wave form, as quantum research postulates. The particle seems to go in and out of state simply because of its interaction with the background energy field (a.k.a. the zero-point field). These zero-point fluctuations might account for "spooky action at a distance," such that every part of the universe relates to every other part. And communication is instant. We refer to this as super position and non-locality—essentially, all particles are always in communication.

The work of Dr. David Bohm is relevant here.[6] He was a student of Robert Oppenheimer, and he postulated that instead of an inert and empty "vacuum" of space, that space was filled with a "plenum" consisting of fluctuating matter and energy. Further, he posited that what we see as matter in physical reality is only a projection—a hologram—of what is really going on with energy and matter. This holographic projection of reality is observed and interpreted by our neurobiology, and this he called the "explicate order." Bohm posited

---

[5] https://www.newscientist.com/article/mg12416932-700-science-where-does-the-zero-point-energy-came-from/

[6] https://www.researchgate.net/publication/369090287_The_Cosmology_of_David_Bohm_Scientific_and_Theological_Significance

The Light Within

that what was happening with base reality in the plenum, which he also called the "implicate order," contains energy known as as "hidden variables." He further theorized that the universe behaves just as holograms do: that each piece of the cosmos carried the information for the rest of it. This suggests that everything is related to and in contact with everything else. This is likely also true of larger beings like us. We bump and bounce into each other and have a telepathic connection with all things. I might summarize Bohm's ideas like this: there is stuff we don't know about the true nature of reality; what we see with our neurons is not base reality; somehow, we are all connected; and it's good to ponder these ideas.

And this work is supported by studies done by Dr. Fritz-Albert Popp.[7] He performed experiments in the 1980s and '90s showing that animals emit biophotons. The more evolved the animal, the fewer biophotons. Popp found that each strand of human DNA emits about a hundred photons when split.[8] He also found that daphnia (the water flea) and young fish would vampirize weaker fry by stealing biophotons. This work has been done with amphibian and fish eggs, resulting in the stronger eggs killing weaker ones. In addition, Popp and his team learned that various living beings suck photons from the space around them and from each other. This phenomenon might function as an information exchange between living beings. It seems as if we are made of light.

It is possible to connect with other beings, such as people, animals, and plants. It is possible to connect to the Akashic records, planetary bodies, and anything you choose. It is possible to heal yourself and others and download creative and business ideas. It is possible to attract vitality, power, and more energy.

You can curate your biofield to such a lovely, magnetic, and high-minded state that you attract only good and beautiful things,

---

[7] For example, see: https://www.iumab.org/prof-fritz-albert-popp/ and https://books.google.com/books?id=FCGcdk5owyEC&q=

[8] McTaggart, *The Field*, pp. 49–50.

people, and places into your life. In contrast, obscene, negative, low-vibrational false belief states attract challenging things and events.

Now let's look at your wonderful life. Study the list below. I created it as the most straightforward way of crafting successful and enjoyable experiences. This book will introduce you to all these topics so you can enjoy your time here on earth most fully.

1. Magnetize your personal aura and fill your physical body and field with source light (energy, vibration, electromagnetism, power).
2. Put energetic protection around yourself.
3. Affirm good things about yourself, perhaps while looking in the mirror or by charging a glass of water.
4. Watch your mental diet; replace the negative with the positive.
5. Visualize. Imagine what you want in your day and for the next week, month, year, and so on—be they material things or events, character and other virtues, or confidence and poise.
6. Along the way, do your personal inner work.
7. Each day do something in material reality that brings your goal closer.
8. Love something: a pet, a person, the world, God.
9. Live your goals in part to help others.
10. Build up your mind; acculturate yourself. Move from baser things to finer ones.
11. Live your faith each day, whatever it is.
12. Do something tough or scary—something you avoid—daily.
13. Exercise for one to one and a half hours, five or six days a week, as you are able.
14. Eat clean food and water as you see fit.
15. Work to be more wealthy, lucky, healthy, brilliant, and joyful. It's your responsibility.

A Gentle Disclaimer

By following the techniques in this book, it's possible to build a life that is 97 percent amazing. While challenging at times, you will learn to manage the other 3 percent beautifully. Stoicism is an excellent philosophy to manage the 3 percent. This ancient Roman school of thought specializes in facing tough things in life head-on, giving you tools to think, *Well, why not me?* After this initial acceptance, you go about finding the advantage in the situation while also being amused and curious about the challenge. This is a great perspective for facing challenges. The Roman emperor Marcus Aurelius, played so memorably by Richard Harris at the beginning of *Gladiator*, was one of the major writers of stoic philosophy, so you'll be standing on the shoulders of giants when you study it. If you need an introduction, Ryan Holiday, author of *The Daily Stoic*, is an excellent resource to get you started.

One more thing before we begin. If you find any of this too difficult emotionally, you likely have powerful triggers. If you are triggered, lose emotional control, or are experiencing too much pain, may I suggest other work first? If you have a strong belief that you can't do this or that it's too hard, you need to do some personal inner work. We all have inner work to do, and we are all on different paths in different places.

1

THE THREE MINDS

Man is what he thinks all day long.
~Ralph Waldo Emerson

There are three minds within you: the conscious mind, the subconscious mind, and the superconscious mind.

Superconscious Mind

The superconscious mind is your higher self, your connection to Source, the source itself, the soul star, the spirit, the universe, and perhaps the Holy Spirit part of you. It is your god self or connection to God. It connects you to whom you talk to spiritually. This is also known as the *Viracocha*. It is an electromagnetic energy ball above your head, and it is infinitely Sourced. I consider and use this energetic ball as a golden light. Whatever your faith or spiritual base, know this golden light is from Source.

This soul star is fed from the universal, cosmic web of life, and perhaps is part of the great field of energy that makes up intelligent infinity.

Conscious Mind

This is your personality and the logical mind: the part of you that talks, thinks, and decides. The conscious mind makes your to-do list. It comprises 2 to 3 percent of your total mind. It is the charioteer that decides what to do, and it should run the chariot—the subconscious mind (more on that later). It should, but most of us don't know how to use the conscious mind to manage and care for the subconscious mind. We sometimes call this conscious mind the objective mind since it involves the five senses and receives evidence from material reality. The conscious mind reasons through observation, education, and experience.

Subconscious Mind

This is the emotional part of you. The subconscious mind can only receive input, and it accepts information from the conscious mind, good or bad, if there is strong emotion attached. It has no choice. Your subconscious mind knows everything and works best when asleep, dreaming, or drowsy. One might say this is where your emotional heart is, and your heart just *knows*. Your subconscious mind sets up events and conditions in your life. Your subconscious mind runs 98 percent of you. You are not a victim of outside circumstance; in fact, you create your reality.

Now, your current life isn't your fault—no one sat down with little you to explain how it works. Odds are there wasn't anyone who could elucidate because your parents probably didn't know, nor did your teachers. And you are not broken; you don't need fixing. You are perfectly, beautifully you. If you'd like to change your life, however, you must work with your subconscious in a particular way so you can have and experience what you want. Your present reality is a result of your past thinking.

Joseph Murphy wrote a fantastic book titled *The Power of Your Subconscious Mind*, in which he talks about the conscious mind like the gardener, planting thoughts in the subconscious mind all day. Your daily thinking plants seeds all the time in the subconscious: *I hate her; I stink; I can't do anything; I can't run fast; he thinks I'm dumb; I don't have enough money; I'll never find love; my kids are no good; my boss doesn't want to give me a raise; I need to go to college to be worth anything; I can't type.*

Your subconscious mind grows those seeds whether they are positive or negative, reading your thoughts like a biocomputer reads DNA and bringing these thoughts to physical reality in some way. It does not question you. To use another analogy, your subconscious mind simply follows orders like a robot. It doesn't need to know the reason behind those orders or, for that matter, if the orders are even a good idea. It just obeys you. You may currently believe your life circumstances just happen to you willy-nilly, but after reading this book, you'll understand your life is created, one thought at a time. You can begin crafting a more lovely life at any moment, the same way you created the current one. Consider the concept "As within, so without" and understand you can use it to your advantage because the subconscious mind is subject to the conscious mind. If you always say you can't afford something, your subconscious mind will make sure you can't. It will arrange your life so that, no matter how hard you work in 3D reality, you will continue to lack funds for what you want and need.

We can liken the three-minds model to the image of an iceberg in the water. The conscious mind is the part of the iceberg we can see. The subconscious is the part under the water. The superconscious mind is everything else: the water, sky, and so on.

Mental Diet

It is vital that you begin to watch and manage your every thought. As you find yourself speaking negatively, say things like, "Cancel, clear, delete," "Cancel, cancel, cancel," "No, I don't accept that!" or "I do not consent."

"I can't type" becomes "Cancel! I don't accept that. It's all good; I type just fine."

This practice is at once easy and difficult, and you'll forget at first, but with judicious practice, you will keep negative thoughts at bay. It may take some work, but you *can* change your mind. Remember, any thoughts you think or say a lot enter your subconscious and stay there since it has no choice—it must accept it. What you think about yourself and others every day is written in your subconscious. Hence, you need to pay great attention to your mental diet. You may need to practice your inner dialogue quite a lot at first, but you will succeed with daily practice. You can also try sitting quietly for ten minutes and asking, "What hurts?" and let whatever comes up for you be present with no judgment whatsoever. Alternatively, you can take everything that gives you feelings of guilt, shame, depression, or anger and put it all on a list. Next, I'll describe what to do with that list.

Quantum Rewiring—Managing Trauma

This is the subject of another book I plan to write, but I want to mention it here so you can use it to help you. I recrafted many energy healing techniques into a system I call quantum rewiring, which uses easy scripts to speak to the higher self and dissociated personality parts. Dissociated personality parts are aspects of you that felt hurt at some point and dove deep into the subconscious, and it's these parts that act up when you get triggered. When these parts get triggered, they can take over your normal, reasonable self and "act out." To assist with this, I use specific scripts to remove the emotional trigger of a painful memory, event, or trauma; if you want to try my method on your own, visit the link below and watch the video at the top entitled *Quantum Rewire Training*.[9]

Then, as each trigger or painful or angry thought comes up, say, "Higher self, do you see the feeling/thought/emotion I have here? The one where I feel such and such? Please tag and treat this and do a massive change history and everything, as needed. Please treat the parts and help them reintegrate to the personality."

If you try this at home, you will feel better. The process is interesting because, for many, energy work like this comes easy. However, if you find you are stressed doing this at home, you will benefit more from a session with me. The steps can't hurt you, and, as I said earlier, it can offer the help you need if you are feeling jammed up with these processes. I also offer coaching to help you achieve your best life.

---

[9] "The Quantum Rewire," The Feeling Better Space, https://feelingbetter.space/quantum-rewire/.

Alternatively, there is help available if you are triggered doing the work presented in this book. Here is a list of things you can research:

- Talk therapy—social worker or therapist
- A life/success coach
- Somatic experiencing
- Somatic breath work
- Reiki and other energy work
- Acupuncture
- Meditation
- Yoga—both the poses and the breath work (pranayama)
- Exercise
- Nutrition
- Neurolinguistic art therapy
- Learning divination tools, such as tarot, pendulum, and muscle testing
- Writing your story
- Journaling
- Emotional freedom technique (EFT, tapping)
- EMDR (eye movement desensitization and reintegration) with a therapist
- Earthing/get out in nature
- Emotion and body codes—Dr. Bradley Nelson

The bad guys

There are entities in this world that don't have your best interests in mind, and I call these elements the "powered elites" or the bad guys. These are the richest and most powerful entities on the planet. While their presence and behavior should not scare you or prevent your success, it is good to be aware that these buggers might try to hinder you. How do they do this? In the physical realm, they tax income, push injurious laws, encourage unhealthy medications, foment division between people and countries, and restrict content on social media. In the metaphysical realm (*meta* means "beyond"), these entities use corporate logos and predictive programming in movies, TV, and mainstream news outlets to get you to think or feel in a certain way. They "program" citizens to feel anger, sadness, anxiety, and depression. And, shockingly, these entities feed off those emotions.

At some level, this is amusing since we joined this game of life to experience things and grow our souls, and so, on some level, we knew what we were getting into. Also amusing is that they are quickly disappearing. There is so much light on the planet that they can't stand it and are leaving the earth plane. However, trapped and injured animals can still be dangerous, and so the world out there can still bite. We can approach our work and development in it with amusement, curiosity, and success, which is why I wrote this book.

The Systems

A mysterious something, mostly invisible until you become sovereign and powerful, doesn't want humans to own their own minds. As a result, when someone starts to think for themselves outside the norm, some serious physical, emotional, or financial blowback will inevitably follow. Vadim Zeland, in his excellent work, *Reality Transurfing*, refers to these somethings as *pendulums*, but I'll use the word *systems* here and explain the phenomenon.

Every group with two or more members—be it an institution, organization, political party, country, religion, racial group, club, family, or even idea—becomes a powerful thoughtform, also known as an egregore, and carries energy frequency patterns of its own. It is alive at some level by virtue of the dynamic interactions between all the minds involved. As the members of the group grow in number and the organization becomes more complex, the power of the system also grows as it takes and feeds on the energy of the members and begins to demand certain behaviors from them.

A friend once told me, "If you make a god, you'll have to worship it—or you'll be punished." The systems function like this.

If the system in question is a senior aquacise club, it may not have that much power. However, an entire religion, country, or political party with more members and intensity does. Systems like this feed on participation paired with lower emotions and conflict, so when the members of a particular group leave or ignore the reinforcing chatter—the guilt, the shame, the anger, the "bad guys who aren't us" narratives, and all the other noise that keeps the circus going—that system falls apart. As members self-police with increasing ruthlessness, the painful emotions created further feed that system. Systems of all sizes and complexities vie for members and for energy, so they fight each other. Political parties fight, and countries wage wars. Systems don't want to die, so they create new reasons for existing. Depending on how you become sovereign, a system can beat you up.

The more you act up, shout, and cause a ruckus within a system, the more it takes notice and can punish you. I knew an army chaplain years ago who was deployed to Afghanistan. He was, ironically, a peacenik and would preach on Sundays against war and the use of drones, and his message was shared with soldiers and marines who had to go out on Monday and wage war and use drones. Afghanistan was, until the very end, a combat zone, and service members were shot at every day. To no one's surprise, the chaplain was scolded and shipped home—he clearly was not a good fit for the army. Whether he was right about drones and war is not the issue, but he chose to jump ugly into the belly of the army beast, and the army system beat him up. How can you advise warriors not to fight when fired upon? He has a beautiful career in ministry now, but the army gave him hell back then.

So how do you beat the systems? You can't destroy them single-handedly unless it's the aquacise club, and we have systems everywhere that we cannot avoid, such as corporations, banks, the medical industry, the IRS, national and local legal systems, et cetera.

You need to learn to play within them using behavioral aikido. When you want to leave a system and be sovereign, this must be played well. The system does not always let you leave without pain or even leave at all. Faced with a change from the system, you need to play it smooth or play it strange.

Play It Smooth

If your boss gives you a task, and you know it's silly or wrong or you know how to do it better, don't tell them that right away to their face. Say, in a neutral and friendly tone, something like, "Sure thing, let me take a look, thanks." Later, approach your boss and kindly and neutrally suggest a few changes or a better person for the work. This way, you are not punching the system right in the face. You're doing it smoothly. My teacher Alberto Villoldo told us we could jump in and fight in these situations for sport, but just to know what we were doing. If the fight is with family at Thanksgiving, you have a fighting chance, but I don't recommend this with the army, a corporation, or the government; it will win. I'm not suggesting caving in to the system's wishes. I'm suggesting you play it smart. There may be things you end up having to do anyway, but there may also be some smooth ways to play it to make it more of what you want.

Play It Strange

Zeland describes a scene in which ten or so bullies were harassing a man who was traveling alone. The man knew he could be killed, so he chose to act very strangely; he told the leader of the group he would rip off his ear. He rushed at the ringleader and tried to grab the ear. Our traveler yelled and jumped around like a crazy person, and his insane behavior caused the group to eventually back off, fearing for their own safety.

I have my own strange example. I was once in the Wingmen's Motorcycle Club House in Fayetteville, North Carolina, on a night when they opened their club to guests. While not a one-percenter club—in other words, an outlaw club—the Wingmen come close. This group is intimidated by no one. I was there with a friend of mine, who had insisted we go. We were at the bar, and at one point, a man walked up to me and said, "We think you should take off your top."

"Uh, that ain't happening," I retorted.

"Well, all the women here have, and if you do, it's free drinks for the rest of your life. Otherwise, you buy everyone in here a drink."

I was contemplating why I'd ever go back there for a free anything, and I had to think fast since I intended to remain fully dressed. I looked at my friend. She just shrugged and admitted, "I did it."

I looked over at two other ladies at the bar, and they said, "Yep, we did it."

I was stuck.

I pulled sixty dollars out of my pocket and put it in the tip jar. I said, with a huge, well-meant smile, "I want to thank everyone here for being so welcoming to new guests to your clubhouse. Thanks so much. I feel very welcome."

They seemed to sense the logic in this and let me off the hook.

2

BASELINE WORK

As within so without
~Hermes Trismegistus

Let's begin with an exercise. Stand in front of a mirror and look at yourself. This provides an initial baseline.

Exercise 1—Baseline Mirror Work

Give yourself thirty minutes and look at yourself, clothes on. See yourself as others may see you. What do you present to the world? Ask yourself these questions:

- What kind of person do I project to the world?
- What do people see when they look at me? Is it different from the way I see myself?
- Am I a villain or a hero?
- Do I project the image of a successful person?
- Do I show a happy personality, or am I gloomy, sad, and negative in appearance?

- Do I slouch when I sit or walk, or do I hold my posture as if I am wearing a crown?
- Are my facial muscles drooping in a perpetual frown, or are my cheeks uplifted as though I am about to smile?
- Do I project charm in my personality, or am I indifferent and aloof?
- Do I have a friendly, loving attitude toward others, or am I hostile and unfriendly?
- Do I project confidence or low self-esteem?
- Do I project a sense of relaxation or tension?
- Am I the type of person I would like to know and have as a close friend?

Now you have your baseline to consider. Many of my clients hate looking at themselves at the start, and this set of questions helps them identify their growing edge. I recall a few years ago when I was doing a yoga teacher training certification, and we were required to wear snug clothes in front of a mirror. I did not like that. I did not care to see my muffin top peeking over the pants—yuck. But it was a real accounting of who I was. I began to accept what I saw, trimmed down, and fell in love with my meat suit. As you do this exercise, you will see that you can change anything you want about yourself.

Have you ever noticed that odd feeling when a person stares at the back of your neck? You just know, and you turn around. Where does that come from? It is because someone is poking into your field, and you can feel it. This is exactly what we are talking about—you can design and craft your own field to be and feel exactly what you want.

How do you wish folks to sense you? Here's a neat trick: I teach a concept I call "owning the room." You can intend to energetically be the most powerful person in any space. First, you do the work presented here in this book, and you set your biofield and intention to own the room before you get there. In this feeling space, you walk in with utmost confidence. Everyone looks at you when you walk in, and they are impressed and want to hear what you have to say. It works easily and well. I recommend that you set your energy to be half a step below that of your boss or military commander since they will sense this, and it will really annoy them.

Exercise 2—Your Part in the Movie

Think about and write down what part you'd like to play in this great movie called life. Do you want to be radiant, energetic, powerful, and magnetic? How about brilliant, talented, successful, charming, and happy? You will begin to move from negative ways of thinking and beliefs to positive and vibrant ones. As like attracts like—and as within, so without—you'll create a more alluring and confident aura. You will attract people, events, and abundance that match your new biofield and your best self. In fact, your positive thoughts will create a fresh, beautiful timeline or parallel reality for you.

What type of life do you want to create for your health, career, lifework, love, and home life? Get a notebook, place these topics as headings, and begin to think big. What do you want to accomplish this week? This month? The next six months? This year? The next five years? You can always change it, and writing it down begins the process of attraction. Set it up something like this:

This Week

- Health/fitness
- Money
- Career/lifework
- Love (family, romance, friendship, country, God)
- Home Life
- Fun

This Month

- Health/fitness
- Money
- Career/lifework
- Love (family, romance, friendship, country, God)
- Home Life
- Fun

The Next Six Months . . .
The Next Year . . .
The Next Five Years . . .

With this, you'll get started. We will do more of this later.

Exercise 3—Daily Mirror Work

Now you will begin to stand in front of the mirror in the morning and say the sentences below or something like them. Do this for thirty to sixty seconds. You may change the wording; be sure the words you choose are bright and positive.

- I am a hero in my life; I have a beautiful destiny. I feel, think, and act as the person I am meant to be, the person I wish to be. I am a person who can have everything I desire.
- I present a happy, smiling face to the world and magnetize friends and loved ones in friendship and harmony. I help others, and others help me.
- I present a prosperous and successful atmosphere around me. I think, look, talk, and act as though I am already a great success.
- I build the magnetic qualities of happiness and optimism and radiate good cheer to everyone I meet.

- I walk tall, with head held high, and I act with nobility, honor, and dignity. I am poised, confident, calm, and serene in every situation. I show strength of character and definiteness of purpose.
- I am joyful and happy, knowing that life offers me exciting new experiences and wonderful things.
- I am the luckiest person, reality is rigged in my favor, everything always works out for me, and everything always happens for me.
- Everything I touch turns to gold.
- Wonderful things are always happening in my life.
- I am the most beautiful/handsome person. I am the most brilliant person.
- I am filled with the consciousness of success and riches to attract money, goods, and abundance.
- I radiate thoughts of happiness and optimism today; my actions shall be positive and courageous. I overcome all tendencies to discouragement and negativity.
- I think thoughts of health, youth, and vitality, and I am filled with a life force that can keep me healthy and young.
- I magnetize my life with qualities of peace, truth, love, and beauty, and these forces of attraction now work in my personality.
- I always have the best day ever.
- Every day, in every way, I am getting better and better.

Congratulations! You are doing inner work and creating new neural pathways that will bring you much benefit.

Life is beautiful and fun, and I invite you to jump in and enjoy it.

Mindset Redux

Watching and curating your mental diet are imperative. This bears repeating. As you are able, and as you remember throughout the day, whenever you speak or think badly about yourself, catch and stop it. When you say negative things to or about yourself, you are basically casting a spell of continuance. What you think a lot about yourself and others *must* enter physical reality.

Thoughts are things, and they travel faster than the speed of light. What you think today is your reality timeline tomorrow, especially if you have an emotional response to your thoughts. I have a funny example from my own life. I never learned to type properly when I was in high school. I was part of the first year women were allowed to take shop class, so, being a brat and a tomboy, I took all the automotive and woodworking classes and happily avoided the cooking, sewing, and typing ones. To me, learning to use a lathe was much cooler than sewing a shirt or typing a paper, so my typing is now a rapid hunt-and-peck style. I currently type constantly, so I often flub at the keyboard, and I'll say, "I can't type!"

And guess what? I'm "cursing" myself to type poorly when I do that. A light, easy example and a true one.

Exercise 4—Mindset Work

1. When you are negative about yourself (or others), say "Cancel, cancel, cancel" and replace the thought with a positive statement. Or say, "Cancel, clear, delete."

   For example:

   "I'm too old and wrinkly to find love."

   "Oh. That's interesting/funny/amusing. LOL, cancel, cancel, cancel."

   "I am beautiful and wise at any age. People love me."

2. Even if you don't believe your new phrases at first, you soon will. You will project this into your subconscious and your biofield, and people will sense it. My friend Joe once said, "Hey, don't talk bad about my friend Liz" when I was annoyed with myself for spilling some coffee. I liked that.

Exercise 5—The Elimination List

Here is another exercise to remove some ill-serving thoughts you are having about life and about your goals.

1. Throughout the day, take note of thoughts that don't serve you, like the sort mentioned above. If some repeat often, jot them down. Or sit quietly for a few minutes with a journal and a writing instrument and ponder which thoughts bother you the most.
2. Create a list of these bothersome thoughts. Write down all the loudest negative thoughts that limit you: *I can't have that, I'm no good, nobody loves me, I'm not strong enough, I'll never have the money, I'm just always sick*, and so on. It does not matter if you feel they are true in your reality; the point is they are negative. The more negative thoughts you have during the day, the more negative your life will continue to be. I'd keep a few copies of this list.
3. Now that you have the list, you can do a few things with it. You can declare to yourself that these are over and done with and burn them safely in a fire. You can do this outside, which is the most fun, or you can use smaller bits of paper one thought at a time and burn them using a candle. Sometimes I like to light a candle inside or have a fire outdoors, and I'll fetch a small stick, sit thoughtfully for a moment, and breathe or blow my negative thoughts and emotions into the stick. I will then burn them in the fire

with the intention that the ill-serving thoughts and emotions dissolve in the flames. When I do this, I find that I "load" the stick with four to five thoughts, and then it seems "full." Follow your intuition.

4. You can also use your list to craft positive statements that will help unravel and dissolve those negative thoughts. To do this, look at one limiting statement at a time and, with intention, cross it out. Go to another page and write out a 180-degree opposite statement. Use that as one of your positive affirmations here in this book. So "I'm always sick" becomes "Every day in every way, I am getting better and better" or "My body is healthy, powerful, strong, fit, and gorgeous."

Now that we have started with a few preliminaries, let's get to the golden circle! This is your personal quantum magnetic aura. While there are many ways to change, grow, and achieve what you want, this system is direct and easy, so I recommend the practice.

If you have not done any visionary or intuitive work, you'll find the following encouraging. First, your biofield can be and has been called various things—notably, luminous field, aura, personal field, your field, and magic circle—and I may use all these terms. Also, when I guide you through visionary work such as the exercises we will do below, know you are truly doing *work*, that something is happening. The work and the change are real. You are mostly energy, and things really are shifting, even if you can't tell with your five senses right now. This is not simply daydreaming. Also, if you do not get good mental pictures when you close your eyes, don't worry; you will develop those skills. For now, simply intend that these events are happening in your mind, and they are. You can also intend or ask that you see pictures and images in your mind more clearly, and you will begin to see more and more. The guidance and steps I lay out for you here are also not prescriptive, so if you want to change the wording and steps, feel free to do so. You are sovereign, so do what you want. Lastly, developing and trusting your intuition will go through "crawl," "walk," and "run" phases. If you already have a Spidey sense, great! If you have never trusted or relied on your intuition, begin by asking yourself, "If I could see or I could know . . . what would I hear, say, or be?" Trust that and go with it. This is how we do it.

3

BEGINNING ENERGY WORK

"Every thought, action, decision, or feeling creates an eddy in the interlocking, inter-balancing energy fields of life. In this interconnected universe, every improvement we make in our private world improves the world at large for everyone."

~David Hawkins

Exercise 6—Your Magnetic Aura

Sit comfortably with your feet mostly on the floor and your back mostly straight.

Breathe in for a count of four, hold the inhale for a count of four, exhale to a count of four, and hold the exhale for a count of four. Do this at least twice. Read these instructions a few times and record them or do them from memory:

1. Count down from three to one, gently and slowly. As you say three, know and feel your body relaxing. Know you are

safe and comfortable. As you say two, know your mind is now relaxing. Any thoughts you are thinking merely float by, and you notice them like ticker tape flowing past your mental screen. As you say one, know you are utterly relaxed.

2. Now, count backward again from ten to one, relaxing even more. As you count, know that each time you do this, you are more quickly and thoroughly relaxed.

3. "Ten, nine, deeper and more relaxed . . . eight, seven, even deeper . . . six, more and more relaxed . . . five, four, more deeply relaxed than ever before . . . three, two . . . so calm and peaceful . . . one."

4. In your mind's eye, create a beautiful golden ball about the size of a beach ball hovering eight inches above your head; then imagine it filling with a golden light. Fill the ball to bursting. This golden energy is a plasma created by Source, and there is an infinite supply of it. Sometimes you see this plasma as little golden squiggles when looking at a blue sky on a sunny day (not into the sun, of course). When you feel a tingling, a warmth, or a heaviness on top of your head, you know you've got it, but don't worry if you don't feel anything since it will come with practice.

5. Send this energy down into your head, then to your neck and shoulders and down your arms all the way, and have it flow out of your hands. Imagine sending any energy you don't need, such as pain, illness, or negative energy from wherever, out of your body. Anything that is not you, you don't need. Push it out.

6. Continue sending the energy down into your chest and belly; then fill your pelvic bowl with it and send it down both legs, hips, thighs, knees, calves, shins, ankles, and feet. See the negative energy leaving from the bottoms of your feet and toes.

7. Sit for a minute and fill your entire body with this golden light, as much as you feel you want. Sit with this energy,

imagining it pushing out anything that your body does not need: bugs, parasites, unwelcome energies, anything. Let this golden light fill your body with strength and vitality.
8. If it feels right, begin to imagine the golden energy at your skin and feel it sparkle.
9. Now, concentrate your energy in your third chakra—the space just below your diaphragm—imagining a golden energy ball filling this part of your body with pulsing vitality. The golden energy from before may still be flowing through your system, and you are now filling this section with extra golden light.
10. When this area feels very powerful and full, send this energy six feet outward all around. Do this gently or with force—however it feels right. Fill your biofield with this golden light, and imagine it removing anything you don't need from your personal field. Build your golden magnetic aura and enjoy it for a few moments.

You are creating something real, not just daydreaming. That said, however, your golden aura may dissipate over time. Thoughtforms just do that. Rebuild your quantum golden field once or twice each day with an intention that it lasts twenty-four hours. It will grow stronger over time and last longer. And if it's fun, you can place a golden crown on your head!

If you have an illness or an area that hurts, use this golden energy to fill the area, imagining the area being healed and free of pain. Reiki masters and other energy healers use this Source light in healing, and so can you.

Your magnetic aura does not have to be golden in color, so feel free to make it any spiritually cool color you like. (When I say *cool*, I mean blue, green, or purple, per the color wheel. White or silver works, too.) If you have not done this sort of work before, go ahead and make it golden. A nice gold color feels cleanest to me, and it matches the golden sky squiggles from Source.

Exercise 7—Grounding and Running Energy

This is important to explain, as I want you to know about one of the basic energy exercises available. You don't always need to do this, but it is helpful, and it's another way to manage your biofield. This exercise does many of the same things as Exercise 6, but this focuses more on grounding into the earth and on energy flow in the body. Try both and enjoy.

1. Sit comfortably with your feet on the floor and your back mostly straight.
2. Breathe in for a count of four, hold the inhale for a count of four, exhale to a count of four, and hold the exhale for a count of four. Do this at least twice. Read these instructions a few times, and record them or do them from memory:
3. Count down from three to one, gently and slowly. As you say three, know and feel your body relaxing. Know you are safe and comfortable. As you say two, know your mind is now relaxing. Any thoughts you are thinking merely float by, and you notice them like ticker tape flowing past your mental screen. As you say one, know you are utterly relaxed.
4. Now, count backward again from ten to one, relaxing even more. As you count, know that each time you do this, you are more quickly and thoroughly relaxed.
5. "Ten, nine, deeper and more relaxed . . . eight, seven, even deeper . . . six, more and more relaxed . . . five, four, more deeply relaxed than ever before . . . three, two . . . so calm and peaceful . . . one."
6. Imagine the cosmic central sun (the center of the universe), if you can, or our own sun sending down a white or golden light into the top of your head.
7. Fill your brain with it and send this light down your spine.
8. Imagine this cord of light moving down to the center of the earth. You may imagine it moving out of your body through

the floor, cement, dirt, sand, water, oil, or anything you like, all the way down to the center of the earth. With your intention, lock it in place at the earth's core and intend to "turn it on" so that anything that isn't you or that you don't need goes down that light tube into the earth.

9. Next, imagine a beautiful earth energy coming up into your feet. Feel it flow through your ankles, calves, shins, knees, thighs, and pelvic bowl and down the light cord heading into the earth.
10. This energy often feels heavier than energy from the sun. You can see if it has a color.
11. Now, intend that, in your pelvic bowl area, the energies blend with a 90:10 mix of sun energy to earth energy. Send this up the front of your body and out the top of your head.
12. Let this energy flow at the outer edge of your aura or biofield. As the energy mix flows down, send it back up the center of your spinal cord area.
13. Imagine a doughnut or toroidal shape. Now, imagine that energy flowing like icing outside the doughnut and returning up the inside of the doughnut hole and back down.
14. If it resonates, you can imagine the flow entirely filling your body and field.
15. Like a slow cooker, you can set it and forget it for twenty-four hours or so. Check on it during the day. Once you do this a few times, you can come up with key words like "shields up" to get this in place quickly and easily.

This is grounding and running energy, and it's the first thing I was taught by the shamans.

Exercise 8 — Chakra Balancing

We can start this meditation the same way. *Chakra* is the Sanskrit word for "wheel" or "circle," and these are energy wheels or spinning energy centers in the subtle body. There are seven major chakras, and these govern major aspects in life. The goal of chakra work is to reach union with the divine. There is much information available about chakras, and I recommend a great book by Asana Swami.[10]

In brief, the base, or root chakra, refers to who you are. It is red and located at the base of the spine. It represents safety, security, basic needs, and survival. The second is orange and reveals how you feel about yourself. It is located below the navel and above the pubic bone and refers to creativity, pleasure, passion, relationships, and sexuality. The third wheel, the solar plexus, is yellow, located below the diaphragm above the navel, and indicates how you think and act in life. This represents your self-esteem and self-confidence. The fourth, your heart chakra, reveals how you love yourself and others, and presents as green. The fifth is known as the throat chakra, is how you express your true self, and it is blue. The sixth is the third eye chakra and is purple. This refers to insight, intuition, and wisdom. The seventh is the crown chakra at the crown of the head and represents enlightenment, spirituality, and divine truth.

When these spinning wheels get out of balance, which happens in the normal course of our lives, we get unbalanced—we may be too materialistic, lack self-love, have low self-confidence, feel great fear or anxiety, are angry toward others, are unable to think clearly, and so on. Let's do a meditation I created for the chakras:

1. Sit comfortably with your feet on the floor and your back mostly straight.

---

[10] Swami, Asana, *Chakra Healing: Techniques to Activate, Unblock, and Balance Chakras for Your Full-Body Energy Cleanse*, self-published, 2023.

2. Breathe in for a count of four, hold the inhale for a count of four, exhale to a count of four, and hold the exhale for a count of four. Do this at least twice. Read these instructions a few times and record them or do them from memory.
3. Count down from three to one, gently and slowly. As you say three, know and feel your body relaxing. Know you are safe and comfortable. As you say two, know your mind is now relaxing. Any thoughts you are thinking merely float by, and you notice them like ticker tape flowing past your mental screen. As you say one, know you are utterly relaxed.
4. Now, count backward again from ten to one, relaxing even more. As you count, know that each time you do so, you are more quickly and thoroughly relaxed.
5. "Ten, nine, deeper and more relaxed . . . eight, seven, even deeper . . . six, more and more relaxed . . . five, four, more deeply relaxed than ever before . . . three, two . . . so calm and peaceful . . . one."
6. In your mind's eye, travel down to your root chakra at the base of your spine. What do you see? Do you see a red ball? Notice if it is spinning, and in what direction. How red is it? It may be bright red, or may be darker or somewhat discolored. Remember, if you don't have inner vision just yet, don't worry, you'll get there. If this is the case, just use your intention and get a sense of what is going on at the root chakra.
7. Now I invite you to correct and improve the root chakra. Intend and make it bright red—your favorite, best red. And intend in your mind's eye that it spin in the just the right way. Once it is beautifully red, enlarge that red color and fill your entire body with this gorgeous red color. Make it bold and red.
8. Now push that red color out to fill your entire aura. Sense that this chakra is cleared, healed, and whole. Feel that it is releasing all memories and situations that no longer serve you.

9. Now go ahead and let that chakra return to normal size, at the base of the spine, perhaps the size of a softball.
10. Let's move now to the second, sacral chakra located a few inches below your navel. This is orange in color. Look, is it spinning? What kind of orange is it? Is it bright or dingy? Using your mental alchemy, make it a vivid orange and encourage it to spin just the right way. Enjoy its bright spin for a moment. It's so healthy and vital.
11. Now expand that wonderful orange to fill your entire body. Enjoy the surging feelings of creativity. In a moment, push that color to fill your biofield. Know that you are releasing energies and memories that are safe to release currently. Let it go back to its normal place.
12. We will repeat all the following chakras in the same way: Move to the third, solar plexus chakra. It is below your diaphragm. See its spin and color. Make it your best yellow and perfect spin. When ready, push it out to fill the body. Push it out to fill your energy field, knowing it is now balanced. Memories and some painful events may be gone or dissolved. Allow it to return to its place.
13. Now move up to the heart chakra. See it. Make it the loveliest green you can imagine. Intend that it spin in a correct way. In a moment, push it out to the entire body. Then, in a moment, still your entire aura. Enjoy the sense of improved love and self-love. Send it back to size.
14. Move to the throat chakra at the base of your throat. Study its color and spin. How is it doing? Create the most wonderful blue for it, and send it spinning the right way. Expand it to fill your body, and when ready, fill the biofield with the blue color. Enjoy a renewed sense of self-expression and personal truth. Allow it to return to its size at the throat.
15. Next, see your third eye chakra between the eyebrows. After studying it, craft the finest purple you can imagine for it. And improve the spin, if necessary. Enjoy its expansion into

your entire body, and moments later, your entire field. Feel refreshed with enhanced intuition and healing of anything necessary.

16. Last, move to the crown chakra, which can be violet or white in color. Check in on it for color and spin. When you see it as the correct color for you, let it fill your body, and when ready, let it fill your biofield. Enjoy a more powerful connection with the divine. Move it back to size.
17. After enjoying this meditation and balancing, relax a moment. When ready, come back to the room and open your eyes.

4

SPIRITUAL PROTECTION

> For with authority and power he commanded
> the unclean spirits, and they came out.
> ~Luke 4:36

One way to put your golden magic aura to work is as protection for you from nasty thoughts sent your way, bad feelings from others, and possible "intrusive fields." Intrusive fields are energies that are not you and not yours, and these don't need to be in your space. I wouldn't worry about this too much—someone wise once said that it's not spirits you need to worry about; it's humans.

Energy vampires are folks who don't make energy on their own, and they love to feed on yours. Your local vampires may be actual sociopaths, in which case, they do it knowingly; but most of the time, these are weaker people who are too lazy or don't know how to make their own energy. These rascals can suck the life right out of a biofield and especially love being around magnetic people.

If you have these people in your life, or nasty people thinking or saying bad things about you, you can push them out of your field using the following techniques. You know when you're around vampires if you feel weak, tired, or annoyed in their presence. Reduce contact, if possible, and build up and shield your energy if you must be near them.

I have a personal rule: I do not take anyone's energy, and they cannot have mine.

Exercise 8—Managing Awful People

1. Do this as soon as you sense something is off about a person. You don't like them, or they don't like you. Please do not let the situation get so far that you have many angry, frustrated, hurt, or anxious thoughts about someone. This is level one work; you can go to the next exercises if things are more troubling. This is a first-pass, early sort of exercise for when you first notice something is off.
2. Sit quietly and comfortably however you like to do it best. Practice the first steps alone while imagining the person in your mind's eye.
3. Imagine all the dark thoughts you have about this person—the things they did or said, what you did or said, how you feel—and place them into a ball of golden light inside your field. You want to gather up all the thoughts in one place in this way.
4. Move this golden ball fifty yards/meters from your space and mentally blow it up. You may need to do this a few times and repeat it for a few days. You want to get to the point where you have an empty space in your field where they are not. This is mindset work. You are not harming the person; you are removing their energy.
5. In a neutral, emotional space, project kind and loving thoughts toward them—for example, thinking that you'd like to meet them. Say to them in your mind that you're so happy to see them again.

6. Do not project unkind or harsh thoughts toward them. Do not try this exercise if you cannot be neutral.
7. This gets you ready for when you do meet them face to face. As you see them, look at the space between their eyebrows—their third eye—and smile. Do not look into their eyes, as they can be defensive, but you can look at them directly by looking at their third eye.
8. You do not need to chat with them; you can simply give them a broad smile and pass them by. In other words, you can keep walking. You realize this person is not disturbing you. They will respond better in the future. You are not shaken in any degree; you are a cool customer.
9. I have found that this obnoxious person might become your best ally and will end up helping you a great deal.
10. If you are too emotional or triggered to do this, the situation has gone too far, and you may need to work on yourself with some of the therapies I mentioned earlier to become more emotionally neutral. You can also try the methods below.

Exercise 9—Protection—Defense

For this exercise, create your golden biosphere, then intend that it pushes out anything you don't need and keeps it out of your space. This intention may be all you need, but you can add to it if you feel you need something stronger. For instance, imagine a liquid mirror reflecting anything you don't need or that's not nice back to the sender. You can choose to send back the same level of energy sent to you. You may suggest it send back four to ten times stronger than it came at you. Your choice. Some of my clients prefer to make the edges of their field a disco ball with tiny mirrors that reflect what they don't want. Alternatively, you might place giant roses all around the edge of your aura. You might choose one single rose or many, and these can be any color you prefer. Check on your roses, your mirror, or your disco ball once or twice throughout the day, and see if they need refreshing. Some of my clients report that their roses wither somewhat or their mirrors look a bit cracked during the day. Use your intention and mental alchemy to refresh and repair what you see. This is kindergarten-level protection yet powerfully effective. Let's go deeper.

Additionally, you might place a brownish, dusty energy cloud outside the liquid mirror to conceal yourself. Intend that you are invisible, and you shall be.

Clients also enjoy surrounding themselves with sacred geometry. Try placing yourself in a purple-colored pyramid or even a purple or golden Merkabah. You can see a Merkabah below; this is two pyramids stacked base to base (one is upside down) and shoved into each other such that each pointy bottom sticks out one of the sides of the second pyramid. You can place a giant Merkabah around your space. Intend that it is there, and it will be.

Exercise 10—Protection—Offense

Do you sense something coming at you energetically when you have had enough? You might choose to go on the offense. After creating the golden ball above your head and filling your entire body, third chakra, and biofield with it, sit for a moment. Next, move even more of that energy into your head and swirl it around counterclockwise until you feel this energetically. Next, place a shield of this light right in front of your third eye (between the eyebrows) for protection. Picture this any way you wish.

Now, know that you can check out the negative energy and see what it is. To do so, send a strong beam of golden light from your third eye through the shield to the negative energy. Your energy will know where to find it; just intend that it goes to the correct place. Next, visualize pulling on that cord of light so whatever the negative energy is comes closer so you can see it, but it remains outside your field. This is not harmful unless you are nervous about it. If you choose to do this, be a baddie and do it. I tend not to be curious, so I don't look; I just take care of it. You have the option to do either or both.

Now let's tackle the negative energy. On the other side of the shield, send a powerful blast of light to whatever it is as a warning. Then say inside your head or aloud, "Go away!"

If you feel it again the next day, send a more powerful blast on the other side of your shield, shouting mentally or verbally, "Go away!" Be louder.

Sometimes we feel an ache in our head or solar plexus, which may be someone sending something unpleasant. Again, sometimes this is a conscious act, but usually it's someone thinking or saying bad things about you or feeling jealous. If you feel an ache somewhere, add extra golden light to the area of pain and place a shield between you and the pain.

There is no need to be anxious about this. It's just energy, and people do stupid things. Keep your field strong, develop your intuition, have a good attitude, and you will be fine. Go get 'em!

If you feel the need for something stronger, first use some of that golden Source light to put up a shield for protection by doing the full exercise. And here is the .50-caliber weapon—send your powerful golden beam of light to whatever the energy is and surround it in a ball of golden light. Then gradually make that ball smaller and smaller until it is one photon, and then have it disappear. You now have destroyed the energy, not the sender. Do this every day until you sense it's gone. Another idea is to surround that energy, move it far from your field, and blow it up. I suggest you use this technique only if you are under serious attack, since this may cause blowback for you. If you believe in karma, there is probably karma.

5

CHARGING YOUR MAGNETIC BIOFIELD

> The world is a mirror, forever reflecting what you are doing within yourself.
> ~Neville Goddard

So far you have thought a little about who and what you want to be, created a golden ball around yourself, and know how to protect yourself. Now let's charge your magnetic field.

Exercise 11—Powering Up Your Magnetic Field

Start with Exercise 6, as previously described.

Sit there with a golden body and begin to visualize pulling in attributes you wish to have. Pull in virtues and character, desires, dreams, and stuff. You can use the various excellent affirmations in this book or your own. I often just pull in words; here is an example of my list: love, joy, ecstasy, happiness, contentment, fulfillment, great riches, fun, abundance, great things happen every day, health, beauty, youthfulness, getting younger every day, brilliance, I'm the best, the greatest, successful at all things, attract romantic love and wealth. Fitness, getting better in every way and every day, doing great yoga, running five miles, ability to heal and counsel others, increasing super psychic intuitive abilities, the funniest person, say the right thing the right way at the right time. Magnetic, attractive, charismatic, amazing travel vacations and experiences.

Just imagine qualities, material things, or events into your golden body. Fill it to the brim. Bathe in the good feeling there for a few minutes. Then you can pull some extra energy into your solar plexus (third chakra). When you are ready, you can push the golden light out into your entire aura and fill it with all those desires and wishes. Modify this exercise any way you like. Sometimes I don't fuss with the solar plexus and just push the light and fill my personal field.

This is incredibly powerful and the key exercise in this book. Do this every day for thirty minutes if you can. You can do it in front of the mirror and also charge your water this way. Simply hold a glass of water, intend all the great things you want into the water, and drink it.

You can add love, truth, beauty, integrity, strength, honor, brilliance, genius, importance, attraction. You can add fun, love, abundance, money, riches, wealth, health, fitness, fun places to visit, fun vehicles to drive. You can add in people you want to meet or influence—people who can help you in your career.

I also suggest that you begin to acculturate yourself. By this I mean listen to refined music like classical or jazz. Read established authors; read biographies of great people. Learn some poetry; feast your eyes on fine art. Good comedy that makes you laugh is wonderful, too, yet this is often profane. If this resonates with you, avoid obscene and profane media, places, and events. Stuff happens, and people get ugly, certainly, but you don't have to watch *every* dystopian movie. As a rule, move toward high-mindedness, high standards, and good laughs. Like attracts like, and you attract what you are.

Exercise 12—Move It into Your Aura

Again, here are some affirmations for you to place in your field. Now, instead of being in front of the mirror, you can sit comfortably in the morning and say these out loud or quietly to yourself. I get up early enough to make time, grab a warm cup of something to drink, and do this myself. Feel free to change or add to this list.

- I am a hero in my life; I have a beautiful destiny. I feel, think, and act as the person I am meant to be, the person I wish to be. I am a person who can have everything I desire.
- I present a happy, smiling face to the world and magnetize friends and loved ones in friendship and harmony. I help others, and others help me.
- I present a prosperous and successful atmosphere around me. I think, look, talk, and act as though I am already a great success.
- I build the magnetic qualities of happiness and optimism and radiate good cheer to everyone I meet.
- I walk tall, with my head held high, and I act with nobility, honor, and dignity. I am poised, confident, calm, and serene in every situation. I show strength of character and definiteness of purpose.
- I am joyful and happy, knowing that life offers me exciting new experiences and wonderful things.
- I am the luckiest person, reality is rigged in my favor, everything always works out for me, and everything always happens for me.
- Everything I touch turns to gold.
- Wonderful things are always happening in my life.
- I am the most beautiful/handsome person. I am the most brilliant person.
- I am filled with the consciousness of success and riches to attract money, goods, and abundance.

- I radiate thoughts of happiness and optimism today; my actions are positive and courageous. I overcome all tendencies toward discouragement and negativity.
- I think thoughts of health, youth, and vitality, and I am filled with a life force that keeps me healthy and young.
- I magnetize my life with qualities of peace, truth, love, and beauty, and these forces of attraction now work in my personality.
- I always have the best day ever.
- Every day, in every way, I am getting better and better.

6

PROJECTING YOUR GOLDEN AURA

To the person who does not know where he wants to go, there is no wind.

~Seneca

You can now charge up and empower your aura to such an extent that you can bring who or what you like into your life.

Mental Movies

First, we need to decide on some goals. We will get to the big goal later.

Exercise 13—Write Down Your Desires

1. Write down some desires exactly as you want them. You will modify this as time progresses, updating your desires and your results. We will get to a big goal, one that seems

impossible, but for now, we are starting gently. Your smaller projects will come along like a large school of fish and will manifest for you along with your huge goal when we get to that chapter. Make a list as long as you want for now.
2. Enter a meditative state, as described earlier, or any way you choose.
3. Ask your higher self, your superconscious mind, or whomever you talk to for advice and guidance on how to improve your project. You can ask for a million-dollar idea, how to get that promotion, or how to create a great business. Ask daily until you get an answer.

If you don't know what you want, sit in meditation for thirty minutes each day, asking for insight from Source and your guides. Also think back to when you were five years old. How did you play? That may tell you your deepest desires and passions.

Exercise 14—Create Your Mental Movies

1. Using the desires you developed in Exercise 10, relax and spend some time crafting short fifteen- to thirty-second mental movies.
2. Then, in the morning, spend ten minutes playing these movies repeatedly. Make these movies feature your desired end, when you have your goal, and you are thrilled. You want to get to the feeling state: how you will feel when you achieve your goal. I usually work with three at a time and imagine them for a bit over three minutes each. Have your movies ready to go (you can jot down the plot), begin to feel the way you'll feel when they're in your 3D reality, and play them in your mind. I offer some ideas next.

Mental Movies for the Right Work

Play the mental movie for the work you'd like to do. See yourself in the corner office with your nameplate on your desk, heading up powerful meetings, and people calling you the boss. Imagine what you do with your success—taking your family on great vacations, starting that charity, helping your brother, or throwing fantastic parties. See yourself at the worksite, watching the beautiful buildings you designed going up. See your paintings on display and being shown and sold in a gallery. See yourself in your career of choice and getting money and recognition for it. See yourself with the record deal or the published book. See yourself giving a talk in front of delighted crowds. Do this daily and follow up on any ideas. You will gradually find and begin to do what you are meant to do. Explore those ideas!

Mental Movies for Finding Love

Be loving and kind. Get good at all kinds of love, such as love for your country and for relatives, friends, and children. Work on a magnetic and romantic aura. Care for your people. Find love in all places. Create short movie vignettes about how you'd like it to be: fun vacations with your person, making dinner together, and great intimacy. See yourself and your person celebrating your one-year wedding anniversary or taking an Alaskan cruise. Imagine them in bed next to you or parking their car in that space in the driveway. Imagine bringing them a cup of coffee in the morning.

Mental Movies for Health, Energy, and Long Life

Your body responds to how you think about it. Create movies that show you living a healthy, long, and happy life. Create a movie in which you are in a fitness competition or doing yoga training. See yourself winning a race, with the T-shirt and the medal. Be motivated to do good work for others, to leave a great legacy. Imagine a scene in which the doctor says you are healthy and fit. See others complimenting you on your youthfulness and your good health.

Mental Movies for Great Wealth

Place the things you want to have and experience in your movies. If you want to send your kids to college or buy them a house, take fantastic vacations, drive a Porsche, or have a beach house, make these your movies. See yourself doing and having. See yourself in your kids' new homes or on that vacation. Imagine driving the car. See yourself talking to the bank teller as he congratulates you on your bank balance while handing you a sheet with high numbers on it, which you read and place in your pocket.

Outside of this exercise, be sure to curate any negative thoughts you have and replace them with positive thoughts. These movies are read by the subconscious, and it goes to work for you. It can't say no to your beautiful acts and affirmations.

Be careful about sharing goals with others. Some may be very negative, and you don't need that; it can detract from achieving your goals. Be sure to share these ideas with people who support and love you. As you grow in your self-concept, this will matter less as you care less and less what folks think of you.

The universe is full and abundant, and there is plenty for you and everyone else. If you do not believe this, it's those bad guys and naive parents and teachers who encouraged you to think that way. You can clean up that thinking. Most wealthy people have money in part because they wanted to offer something to the world. They often started out being poor. They have magnetic personalities and attract and influence people. They have developed a sense of intuition.

Your average wealthy guys or gals have built themselves up with great ideas and determination.

You can make up pretend money and pretend gems, deeds, and stocks for yourself. There is fake money you can purchase online; I play with faux $1 million bills. You can get plastic gems in various colors. You can print up pictures of beautiful homes and make up deeds for property. You can craft paper stocks as well. Some folks have a treasure box they put these things in.

The Abraham-Hicks material suggests you write out checks to yourself for real events and things and make it a thousand more dollars every day.[11] They call it the Prosperity Game. You don't really present these checks, and you don't get the things yet. It is materializing what you wish for. You can create a vision board as well. There are a thousand ways to manifest; after you work through this book, explore!

For another excellent resource, check out *Think and Grow Rich* by Napoleon Hill. His book describes five steps to success:

1. Decide what you want most in life—in this case, how much money and by what date.
2. Decide what you will do for this money and do it; follow any inspired action you have doing the process.
3. Write it down.
4. Create and recite a prayer of gratitude.
5. Read it all twelve times every day.[12]

Create the mental movies discussed earlier. You can use the same techniques for wealth, love, health, and so on. We break it down a bit into chapters, so you have some specific ideas of things to do. All the techniques work for all issues.

---

[11] Hicks, Esther and Jerry, *Ask and It Is Given*, Hay House, Inc., 2004.
[12] Hill, Napoleon, *Think and Grow Rich*, The Complete Classic Text, Tarcher Perigee, 2008, pp. 22–50.

7

ATTRACT AND INFLUENCE PEOPLE

You can make more friends in two months by becoming interested in other people than you can in two years by trying to get other people interested in you.
~Dale Carnegie

You can use your magnetic biofield to attract the people you want into your life. These may be romantic partners, people who can aid your career or business, and a fun tribe of friends. The techniques you've read about up till now already do that, but here, we are focusing on attraction and influencing more directly. First, it is ideal that we work on ourselves. While we live in a time when people insist on being accepted as they are, and this is usually a good thing, we can consider becoming even better people. I don't mean to bug you about yourself here; these are good ideas for your consideration.

Bringing happiness into your life and your field is important to attract others. Life can be sketchy out there, I know, but find a stream of happiness for yourself. Is your garden doing well? Are you warm and dry each day in your home? Do you have some good friends? Can you love your pets or children? Do you have other people to love in your life? Can you make a decent meal for yourself? You may not have all you desire, but there is something, certainly, you can focus on being happy about. I knew a fellow who had been so depressed he could hardly get out of bed each day. I encouraged him to keep trying and keep looking for something to enjoy. He told me at one point that he was successful in getting out of bed and frying himself an egg. He ate it on buttered toast before climbing back under the covers. He had mastered that skill and felt better. He eventually mastered one thing each day, and two years later, he now has a successful photography business. Happiness is not everything, but it is a huge part of being attractive. This is the opposite of being an energy vampire and means you have good energy in your field. People are attracted to that. Remember, you can set up your field so that while you are charismatic to others, no one can take your energy from you. They need to grow their own.

Being as good a person as you can is also attractive. Invoking the virtues you appreciate into your field, such as integrity, truth, honesty, inner strength, and character, will help you be more alluring. Generosity is a great attribute to cultivate. When we are generous, we attract more generosity, and folks appreciate it. Being kind in this way helps us feel good. Kindness adds wonderful energy to the surrounding area. People will be attracted to your light.

I have known some dark magicians. While they have claimed to be happy with their lives, I do notice that, over time, they seem to lose Source energy and energy in general and become people I don't want to be with. They seem darker and darker to me and increasingly unable to look me in the eyes with their own clean light since they have less and less of it. They seemed to get more and more blowback, becoming poorer and sicker. This may not be true of all dark types, but I have noticed this trend among people I know. They suck your energy and feed off it. It is better to avoid these people and not be like them.

I always encourage bringing an inner beauty and radiance into your field as well. We want to share our beautiful souls with others as well as see beauty in all things. It's not the outer skin that people find attractive; it's the inner soul's radiance that brings people in.

Have faith that you are valuable and have a great destiny. Have faith that the Creator has your best interests in mind. Have faith that you can make money doing something you love, even if not right away. Have faith that you are loved and wanted. If you struggle in one of these areas of attractiveness, this may signal something for you to work on. For example, if you don't have the fitness you would like, your next bit of personal work may be learning about diets and body care. This is a spiritual endeavor. If you don't have a good self-concept, this may be an area for you to think about. Don't be too concerned; you have a whole life ahead of you, so pick something to work on and go for it. If you don't like other people or have a hard time relating, perhaps you can learn how to be with people and how to find people you trust and like. You can work on your stuff alone or with a counselor, coach, or friend. Along the way, you can add faith, kindness, and more into your field and ask Source to help you understand better. You're here anyway. You may as well be great.

Love has so many levels to it, and this may be the most powerful and sacred emotion there is. People who naturally radiate love attract many good friends, wonderful events, and opportunities in life. We are not just speaking of romantic love or passion; we are speaking of love for parents, people, country, God, children, animals, the earth, and partners.

Let's talk about your voice. Have you noticed that you are attracted more to people who have mellifluous voices? Those who speak with a whiny, shrill, or nasally voice drive people away. You may want to work with a voice coach or play the musical scale and find where your voice lands in your chest. This is the best timbre for your speaking voice. I once worked with a young female army Specialist. She was doing some work for me, and I gave her the task of emceeing an event and making announcements. Her voice was so shrill that she was driving soldiers out of the room. I pulled her aside and suggested she bring her voice down into her chest, and we practiced it until she was comfortable moving her voice around inside her body. She returned to give our mission information, and the whole room relaxed and paid attention. She was free to speak any way she liked, of course, at any time. But now she had the ability to move her voice, so she sounded pleasant to the ear. It's attractive.

If you have never thought about this before, you can ask someone you know how your voice sounds. You can improve the tones in your voice. You can use your voice as a blessing, and people will respond to you well.

Exercise 15—Watch Your Tone

Work with a musical friend or play a scale for yourself, singing or saying "Do ray me fa so la ti do." Find where your voice sounds comfortable in your chest. My musical pal Sherry says to simply bring your voice down near your heart, and you've got it. Now, at least, you have the skill if you want it.

When you converse with someone, where to focus your eyes is always interesting. I have learned to look someone right between the eyes, in their third eye. You can't look them in one eye at a time; that would look odd. If you look between their eyes, it's as if you are looking at both. Practice this. Occasionally, you can glance away but come back and look at the person with confidence this way. And sit still, but more on that later.

People Skills

Another thing you can do is to make people feel important. Ask them about themselves. Ask about their interests. Ask follow-up questions; don't just wait to say something yourself. As you listen to a person, are you thinking about what you want to say, or are you actively listening? I still work on this since I'm so verbal.

Unless you know the person well, I would not tease or criticize them. There is a whole culture of teasing in the world; our sitcoms are funny, but to relate with someone well, be kind. Every word out of your mouth is a blessing or a curse, so you may as well bless. If you speak blessings, blessings will return to you.

Be truly interested in people. If you are not, this can be some personal work for you. Figure out how to like people. I believe it is useful to introduce yourself confidently and with poise to others who may be too shy to approach you. Try to recall names well, too. I am still working on this. Also, do not boast and brag. It is better to have others say sweet things about you, not you. It is always more impressive that way. Another lost art is thank-you letters. Whether it be in an email or a real snail mail letter, saying thank you does wonders for people.

As I write this, I am thinking of my grumpy and jaded friends who don't care for people and don't want to be nice. I get it. Don't do what you don't want to do. I'm not speaking here of someone not worth your time. I'm speaking here of how to be with folks you find worthwhile. These skills are good to have to pull out of your pocket.

Most topics I bring up are yearlong studies in themselves. This book is a guide to lay out ingredients for a successful life so you can go rock with your bad self in any way you choose. Boundaries are hugely important. It's ideal to know where you begin and others end. It's good to know what's yours and what's not. It's beneficial to understand what you can change and what you cannot.

If you find yourself giving your energy and time away so you are drained or resentful each day or you find yourself bossy and controlling over others, you may want to study the concept of boundaries with people. Boundaries are a huge subject worth a great deal of study. Don Miguel Ruiz wrote *The Four Agreements*, and I highly recommend this work. If you do the practices in that book, you will for sure have great boundaries, protect your own energy field, and have a superb life.

Here is a boundary teaching in a nutshell for you.

What you have control over:

1. Your body and your energy field
2. Kids under 18 of whom you have guardianship and those over 18 if they live with you, and you are paying their bills
3. Your pets
4. Your stuff
5. Your opinions, mind, emotions, thoughts, attitude
6. Your response to everything that happens around and to you

That's it. Essentially, we have boundary issues when we give our responsibilities and rights away to another or try to boss someone around. I have a personal policy of not offering unsolicited advice. If they are not asking, they are not listening.

Remote Sensing/Viewing/Influencing

We have dispensed with the practical aspects of getting along with folks in material reality; now let's do something more interesting. You can use your golden Source energy to connect with people and influence them. If this is new to you, you may need to trust your intuition and let it develop and grow.

Remote sensing and viewing are basically getting a feeling and a vision of what's going on at a location or with a person. Also, I see remote viewing as imagining your luminous body there at the site or with the person. Remote influencing, on the other hand, is giving a person a message or making a request. These techniques require a level of maturity and kindness. If you use them to be mean or harmful, these instructions will not work for you. You will just find yourself in an emotional mess. If you think about it, your thoughts have much power. In a true sense, they are spells. Remember, at some level, any thought you think is picked up by your person. Their higher self and subconscious mind will know. It's just better to become a kind person and curate your thoughts. A righteous and temporary annoyance at something is one thing, and pure harm is another.

The military developed a formal remote viewing program, and some of those techniques are still taught today by great practitioners. This is not what I do and teach. I just go. It's actually very simple. The key is to practice and trust what you get.

Exercise 16—Remote Sensing, Viewing, and Influencing

1. Get yourself to a comfortable alpha/theta state.
2. Do the golden ball exercise over your head and into your body.
3. Do your shielding by extending the golden energy out six feet from your solar plexus. Place a mirror on the outside, and conceal yourself if you wish.
4. Take some of that golden energy and swirl it around your brain. Have it energize your third eye area, and shoot a cord of light from there to wherever you wish. You can go to a place, go see a person, or check on your kids. I would use this with care. If it's the island of Crete you're interested in, go there and walk around. You may not be 100 percent accurate at first, but you will begin to trust yourself and see more and more with practice. I sometimes do this with a partner so we can check each other's accuracy (as in, do we see the same things?). Just imagine yourself there if you intend to view it.
5. If it's a person you are checking on, I suggest you keep the cord at the edge of their field. If they are energetically

protected, you won't be able to get in anyway. You can touch the edge of their field and see how they are doing. Remember, if you believe in karma, there will be karma, so be careful. I would not use this to accuse your friend of anything later. I have used it to sense if a guy is cheating on me, but instead of accusing him in material reality, this exercise helped me decide to leave him. (This was not my only data point.)

6. You can send your person a message using this technique. You can tell them you like them or ask them to call you, message you, stop by, give you an interview, or offer you the job. I suggest you use a kind, neutral, or encouraging voice. Do not yell, demand, or accuse. Be nice, since being negative does not work well for your desires. That is, in fact, what they will pick up on, and they will avoid you. Remember karma and remember blowback. Remote influencing does not always work and sometimes takes time. You can do this twice a day for a week or two. You may need to be patient.

7. You can use this technique to have a conversation with your person if you've had a fight or are not in contact. Again, be neutral and kind: "I am so sorry about our disagreement, and I'd like to work it out. I really wish you well. What can we do about this? What do you think? I wonder if we can try . . ." And so on. You can imagine them speaking to you. What would they say? I have had clients hear volumes from their person. Just trust what you get, and you'll become more accurate. When you speak to them next in 3D reality, it will go better.

8. You can sit quietly with yourself and ask for the best way to bring in money, how to improve a relationship, and so on. If you do this daily for fifteen to sixty minutes, you will see images in your head or receive potent ideas to try. You can also invoke famous people or those with skills you want and invite them into a cosmic committee—discussed later—to

help you. Have conversations with them and ask for inspiration. I have a "safe on the motorcycle" committee that I invoke before I ride. These are the best riders on the planet, and they inspire me while I'm out and about.

9. This is an important one: You can send a cord from your third eye and intend to connect it to Source or God or the universe. You can imagine connecting and asking any questions you like. Ask for insight into a problem. When I do this, I sometimes imagine connecting with the cosmic central sun, which I see as the center of everything. Imagine whatever Source is to you. You may not trust what you are getting for insights at first. Keep asking, and you will get better, improve your intuition, and trust yourself more and more. There is an answer to any question you ask.

10. Practice! You'll get better and more accurate with time. Just do it and assume you're getting something right, and you will improve.

8

IMPROVING YOUR HEALTH

I have spent most of my time worrying about things that have never happened.

~Mark Twain

Doing the golden ball exercise is healthy for your body. The energy you invoke is Source light, and it is healthy. As you bring in the light to your body, imagine it pushing out ill health and any sickness or bodily pain. As previously stated, imagine the light pushing out any intrusive fields in your space. And remember, this, and any visualization for any purpose, does not just change you immediately or seemingly magically. It may take some time. Healing may also come in the form of insights into things to try for better health. It may be a person you meet who can help. It may be a website, a video on social media, or a song. Practicing the processes in this book will change your life, so be on the lookout. And, by the way, it's all magic, which is natural and normal.

You can use many of the techniques already offered in these pages. In this chapter, we will speak about more specific health concepts and issues. Much of this chapter is plainly obvious; it may be challenging for some to implement healthful changes. I do find that quantum magnetism and the use of affirmations can help you have the drive and desire to make any desired changes.

Much of our chronic ill health is psychosomatic. There are myriad resources and studies strongly suggesting this. A powerful resource to review is *The Body Keeps the Score*, by Bessel ven der Kolk. And 80 percent of our illnesses are chronic. This means our mindset affects our health. I would also argue that it's possible—it's *possible*—that our accidents are also created by our subconscious minds. I say this because, on more than one occasion, I have worked with clients who "arrange" accidents for themselves on anniversaries of, say, the death of a child or spouse. It's worth considering that we may cause our accidents; they may not be happenstance.

Shame, guilt, anger, and depression can cause health issues. Some have said that anger can cause joint and especially lower back and hip pain. And depression can encourage cancer growth. I am not a doctor, and this is not medical advice, but that has been my experience and my research. When my clients do their inner work and clear up these darker emotions, their issues often ease. You can certainly aim for wellness with personal work and a mental and emotional diet.

Fear

Fear can adversely affect our physical well-being. I think that most fear boils down to a fear of death. Fear releases cortisol and adrenaline, hormones which, over time, can be deleterious and cause weight gain and other comorbid challenges. A faith-based or spiritual practice can ease fear. For Christian folk, reciting Psalm 23 or Psalm 91 can help. Whatever faith you are, there are probably verses in your good book that will ease fear. Processes in this book, as well as cognitive behavioral therapy (CBT), eye movement desensitization and reintegration (EMDR), and similar practices can help. I have used the emotional freedom technique (EFT) with clients to good effect. Being with a buddy can help. If you are able, I suggest taking one thing you are afraid of and looking at it directly without avoidance. A study of stoic philosophy is useful. Some shamanic practices can help you lose your fear of death, and this can help immeasurably. Your soul is immortal, and realizing this can ease the fear of death.

You can use affirmations like the following:

- I desire vital good health, youth, and energy. My cells and all my body processes work beautifully.
- My body is now healed from any challenges. I now express life, health, youth, and energy and grow strong and healthy.
- I am safe; I am whole; everything works out to my advantage; God is looking out for me; this, too, shall pass; I always figure things out.
- I am full of health, and my body is amazing. My body heals perfectly and shows me what to do. I am so happy and grateful that my body is so healthy and strong. My body grows healthier and stronger every day. Every day I get better at caring for my health. My health is always improving. I am power and health. My problems are being solved, and I am gloriously confident that everything works out for the best. I now release magnetism in my brain and body cells, which strengthens me and overcomes fear, worry, hate, and all other negative emotions. I supplant any negative emotions with confidence, love, and inner peace.
- I now change all negative situations into positive ones.
- Every day in every way, I am getting better and better.
- I am the center of dynamic quantum magnetism and power. My problems are even now being solved, and I am gloriously confident that everything is going smoothly.

I find when I consider and work with affirmations like these, I am inspired to learn more and care for my body in new and powerful ways.

Recalling times in your past when events did work out and sitting with those memories can also help.

Live life fully; go for it. A gutsy, bold life prepares you for death. Change the things in your life you can change, and don't worry about the rest. I had a pastor who used to call worry "borrowing trouble." Why borrow trouble with something you can do nothing about?

If you are afraid and worried, this may be your next bit of personal work, and there are many ways you can go about this. Ill health can also stem from painful emotions. Now, please know that all emotions have purpose and are useful. But if they linger and we do not process and move through them, they can be a detriment to our well-being. Guilt, shame, and anger experienced long term can create illness.

I offer an example: A client told me that her brother sexually assaulted her after he had been out drinking. She stopped the assault before it got too far, but they never spoke about it, and he never apologized. This happened many years ago. Today, his health is terrible. He does not care for himself, dresses poorly, and does not bathe. He was recently diagnosed with esophageal cancer and has gained 150 pounds. He is angry with everyone in his life and has hinted that he has very little will to live. His health situation may be due in part to his terrible moral misconduct and his continued denial.

Your health is also supported by being kind and helping others. Living an orderly life of harmony as much as possible will also help. Doing work that you love can be key, too. Watching or doing things that make you laugh is great. Dancing or singing can do wonders. Working on these good habits over time is wonderful. Some of these concepts are obvious; these are reminders for you to consider what you might work on next.

Also, and it must be said, hard physical workouts for an hour at least five or six days a week and a clean diet (whatever that means to you), as you are able, are beneficial. A daily walk is beneficial as well. You may consider regularly doing some type of fasting practice; there are many kinds. Clean water is important. Avoiding processed foods is beneficial, as is being out in nature—barefoot, if possible. Doing something for your physical health daily is a superb practice. You can begin to implement these practical helps day by day; if you have some physical challenges, it's likely you didn't get there in a day, so be patient with yourself and give yourself time. Get up and do a little more each day. Growth, change, and character are what you do in private—the small things, when no one is watching.

We should also work toward balance in our lives. We need to sleep around six to eight hours, play, rest, and have a balanced work life. One of my teachers said we should sleep one-third of the day, rest/play one-third of the day, and work one-third of the day. I am not sure how reasonable this is, but it is something to think about. Do things in moderation. Another teacher said to put in at least five good hours on your goal or project; you don't need to work overly hard to attain your goals. Work well when it is time to work. I used to have a saying with my kids: we work hard and play hard. This is easy to say and certainly more challenging to do. I have had friends who spent some years figuring out why they didn't sleep. While they were busy with the rest of their lives, sleep was always an issue. I have suggested to them that good sleep may well be their spiritual practice.

Which brings me to another life point: What is the best thing to create balance right now? You may enjoy various hobbies, but your life situation may present you with something to work on now. I often use the example of an extremely unhealthy woman I knew at church back in the day. She had diabetes and COPD, suffered from swollen ankles, could hardly walk, and had heart issues. She was unable to walk or exercise at all. She insisted on making casseroles for the church. She attended PTO meetings at school and ran for local office. She was clearly a civic and spiritual go-getter. Yet I wonder if a better goal and practice for her would have been to look at her health. I understand that there were avoidance and other psychological issues at play, but she might have done better to consider her health. Perhaps Source was offering health as a next exploration for her. Just a thought. We often project outward to the world instead of looking right at home at our own stuff. What is life showing you?

9

YOUR COSMIC COMMITTEE

> The happiness of your life depends upon
> the quality of your thoughts.
> ~Marcus Aurelius

I don't remember where I learned this, but I often hire and use a committee of nonphysical beings. You can ask a committee of angels or some higher beings to form a group and give them jobs. This is for real. Napoleon Hill might call this a cosmic mastermind group.

You can create a set of beings if you don't believe there are any. These will be thoughtforms you send out to do things for you. You can use angels or saints. You can invoke the skills of people, living or dead. You can create a group for a romance committee or a job committee. Give them various jobs, and be sure to carry out any inspired action you feel you should. I know a man who told me once he was so shy, he said, "God, if you want me to get married, you'll have to have her knock on my front door." He married the Avon lady! It *can* happen that this committee or God and your personal quantum magnetism work to bring someone to your front door, but usually, your intentions require some logical or inspired action. Maybe you don't have to do too much, but likely, you will have a few things to get out and do, and some things to work on. I have found that I get jobs more often when people call me out of the blue than when I (used to) vigorously job hunt and send out two hundred résumés. In other aspects of my life, I must hit the pavement a lot. Crazy.

What this does is get the troubles out of your hands. You speak what you want in faith and trust and hand it back to God or to your committee. Then you can stop worrying about it and know it's happening. My teacher Alberto Villoldo instructed us to take whatever was troubling us or whatever we wanted and make an energy ball with our hands and our intention. Then we were to place our concern, desire, or worry into the energy ball and toss it up to the great spirit. We were to say out loud, "Whoosh!" and then toss it up and away and let Source take care of it. If you try one of these techniques, just toss it up or speak to your committee; then forget about it and trust it will happen for you.

Exercise 17—Form Your Committee

1. If you have beings you work with, then enjoy them and continue with that. Speak to them however you usually do and tell them you are starting the "get a job" committee, the "start a business" committee, or whatever you are working on.
2. You can get a notebook and assign specific tasks to specific beings. Or you can tell all of them what you want and to go and do it, like I do. I also ask that they instruct me on any inspired action I can take.
3. You can hold meetings if this resonates with you. You can take your golden energy, send a cord to any of your beings, and ask them how they are doing. Or simply straight up

ask them how the process is going. This is not prescriptive; have fun with it. You are in charge. You can have many committees working on various things. Some people get into shamanic practice or magic to work with these beings potentially more powerfully. Do as you like.

10

COSMIC RHYTHMS AND LAW OF TIME

> The future is a concept—it doesn't exist.
> Time is always now. . . . [T]here is only
> the present, only an eternal now.
> ~Alan Watts

Cosmic Rhythms

There are certain cosmic rhythms in life, and it helps to coast along with these as we steer and direct our desires. Full freedom means we do what we want, when we want. It is also sweet to use our skills, wealth, and desires to help others and make the planet a finer place to live. There is a way to reach higher into the planetary and galactic realms to bring what we want into our lives sooner rather than later while still coasting along the galactic tides. The interstellar clock will continue to click along, but your desires can flow along with it and deliver your desires to you.

For this exercise, I recommend that you plan for the next year and for the next five years. Make a list of all that you want in your life during these time frames. Would you like to get married and start a family? Do you want an Aston Martin in the garage? Your own business franchises? To live somewhere else? To retire and go fishing?

Exercise 18—Playing with Cosmic Rhythms

1. Get yourself to a calm alpha brain state however you want to do it.
2. Create or have your list of your desires. Set a time for when you want to achieve or manifest these desires.
3. Rise above your desires for the moment and spread yourself and your field out into space, the cosmos, right to the very cosmic central sun. Go see and be with what you sense as Source or all that is. Be as large as the universe. Be there a moment. Enjoy that joy, that expansiveness. Be as high vibrating as you can.
4. Visualize your own personal golden sun (your field) around you. See the sun radiating down on the earth, and visualize yourself as that sun, radiating on the earth as well. You are a divine center of dynamic power. You are projecting your own cosmic brilliance out into the universe. You can use the symbol of the sun for this as well; every time you see the sun, know it's you, and you are setting cosmic timing in place.
5. Repeat these statements while you are in this high state:
    a. I am now in tune with the cosmic intelligence that created the universe.
    b. I control the creative power of my mind and now project to this cosmic mind the directions I wish it to carry out on my behalf. (Say or read your list.)
    c. I now set a cosmic time clock for the events and things I desire.

    d. I desire creative mental gifts that will increase all my talents.
    e. I wish to project in my body and my field power, magnetism, and strength, which will cause others to be attracted to me and support me.
6. After you say the above, you can program the higher mind with the events, money, conditions, people, objects, and experiences you wish to have in your life. Do not worry about asking for many different things. You can have a daily list and lists for a month, six months, a year, five years, or longer. These will mature into your life according to the cosmic timing. Enjoy!

Another aspect of rhythm is a sense of poise and calm. If you fidget and play with your face or keys or jiggle your legs, this dissipates energy in your field. You spend your energy and have little left for powerful, constructive personal work. You can practice sitting still with a timer set for a few minutes to begin. Don't play with things on the table or your phone. Do not move your legs. Do not fidget for five minutes or more, and you can work up to thirty minutes. This is a useful skill and one that is not taught much anymore. If you are in a meeting live or online, and you fuss about, others find this distracting, and you lose energy. Practice looking at the speaker right between their eyes for lengths of time. As I said, you can look away now and then so you don't seem too intense and creepy, but a steady, consistent gaze between the eyebrows is best. People will see you differently.

When you do speak, avoid depressing and critical comments. Speak with an encouraging tone. As I said, every word out of your mouth is a blessing or a curse, so you may as well speak blessings. I have friends who enjoy being snarky and love to tease since it's fun for them. I've known these folks for a while, and I just have a sense they'd do even better in life if they spoke kindly to others.

Liz L'Eclair, Ph.D.

Exercise 19—Time Is Not Law—Another Way to Play with Rhythm and Timing

1. Write "Time Is Not Law" on a piece of paper. Also write down everything you want in this eternal now:
   a. $_____ whatever amount you like
   b. A better home of my own
   c. A new car
   d. To build my own business, etc.
2. Know that once you write these down, they are on their way to you.
3. Get into a meditative state in any way you like.
4. See yourself as large as the cosmos and part of it. You are part of this huge cosmic web of life. This universe knows and has all you need. There is plenty for all. Scarcity is a false belief.
5. Ask for guidance and intend to speed up your mind and soul to the level of the vast cosmos. Imagine forces of light, energy, and vibration coming from the great universe toward you, with all you need and want.
6. Be sure to improve 1 percent every day in knowledge and action to get what you want.
7. Repeat these phrases if they resonate:
   a. I now accelerate the rate of vibration in my brain cells.
   b. I create the cosmic whirlpool of dynamic creative action.
   c. I desire power to carry out my pattern of creative work.
   d. I wish to become an artist (or author, inventor, composer, businessman/woman, whatever you wish to be), and I now stir the psychic centers of my higher mind into action.

e. I ask for inspiration to carry out my master plan for the future.

This exercise differs from the prior one, since this is more of a high-vibrating call to the universe, as opposed to expanding and becoming the universe.

11

A REALLY BIG GOAL

> You're going to be here anyway;
> you may as well be great!
> ~Arash Vossoughi

Martha Beck, my former teacher, taught us to dream big, and she referred to this as eagle view. If there were no limitations, what would you dream of doing? If money, education, or life situation did not matter—which, in fact, they do not—what would you do? I find in my coaching with clients that if they aim at 100 percent of whatever they dream about, they reach between 89 and 99.99 percent of their goal, or they change it for something better. Those are decent odds! If you aim for, say, 67 percent, you may get to 65 or 67 percent. Why not aim as high as you can? I remember sitting with a friend on New Year's Eve in 2011. She was teary and miserable. I asked her what she wanted in life.

"I want to learn German in Germany!"

"So why not do it?"

"I can't. My boss won't let me take that much vacation."

"Do you know that? Have you asked? What else could you do?"

"Well, maybe I can ask him for my vacation and offer to take unpaid leave for the rest of the six weeks."

"Sounds great! Go do it, and let me know how it works out."

She came back and said she offered to quit her job, since taking German was that important to her. Her boss let her go to Germany and return to work afterward. She now works at a place that uses her German, and she is thrilled.

By the way, that newfound freedom she exhibited also opened her up energetically for the other thing she wanted: to find love. She was more magnetic and had more personal power, and as she prepared to leave for Germany, she met and began dating a wonderful man. They are married now, and I got to perform their marriage ceremony.

We have addressed setting goals already, but here we want to focus on a big, seemingly impossible goal. What do you truly want—without limits? If you did not need money, what would you do for free? A huge goal is something that you have no idea how you will achieve. Your logical mind may think it's crazy and will have no idea how to get it. This is the point. The how is none of your business. Your subconscious and superconscious minds know how to get it for you. Neville Goddard and many others would say that once you think of what you want, creation is finished. This means what you desire is in your energy or biofield already. You need to become that person who can receive it. You need to vibrate at the level of the reception of your goal. You'll know you have a great goal when your logical conscious mind wants to reject it because it does not seem reasonable.

Exercise 20—Dream Big

1. What do you love? What are you curious about? Look into these. If you love something, there is money in it for you. It can be a challenge to parse out just how, but you can. Some

people feel better having a new goal as a side hustle and not quitting their day job at first. Others jump in fully right away. Do you love saving homeless cats and woodworking, for example? Maybe you can craft and sell *catios*, or catteries. I love healing, coaching, counseling, divination, and writing, so here I am.

2. If you are really stuck, maybe just stay there and continue to dream and plan. Look at images you like: vacations, beaches, homes, vehicles, animals. Ask Source what it has for you; why are you here? Search the internet. Make a commitment to meditate daily until you have some inspiration. Ask your friends what they see you doing; they may have some insight. Collect images for a vision board and write down ideas.
3. Meditate for thirty minutes daily, asking what your right lifework is. Keep at it until you have something.
4. Think back to when you were five. How did you play?
5. Lastly, you can just choose something and try some baby turtle steps in that direction. I recall speaking to a military spouse one time who wasn't sure if she wanted to be a psychologist. She was frustrated, since she didn't know whether to apply for the PhD program or not. She felt she had to swallow the whole pill or not do a thing. I suggested she break it down into exploratory steps that were less scary and carried less investment of time and money. I suggested that she attend a psych class, interview a professor or practitioner, and read psych certification websites to discover the requirements. What did certification look like? The standards of care? You can try the same approach; if you change your mind, think of all the knowledge you'll have.
6. When you have a goal, condense it down to a pithy, concise statement. Say it to yourself in the mirror for five minutes each day, and write it out ten times every day. Chapter 11 has some other ideas as well.

You may not be content until you enjoy your work.

Exercise 21—Self-Confidence

Stand in front of the mirror or in your meditation space and say things like "I am powerful. I am strong. I am amazing. I am confident and brilliant. I am a success. I am the best. I am loved. I came to do a great work."

If you are in front of the mirror, do you feel better than you did the first day?

12

WHAT TO DO WHEN YOU'RE FREAKING OUT

So it's bad right now. The breakup, the divorce, the end of a friendship, the failure, the job loss, the diagnosis, the grief, the loss, the loss, the loss.

We have all been there, and I have some ideas. These tips are simple; the challenge will be to remember to do them. Here is what I suggest:

1. Breathe. This comes first. It calms your nervous system. Take some deep breaths. I'll list some options.
    a. Do the box breath suggested by heartmath.org.[13] Breathe in to a count of four, hold the breath for a count of four, exhale to a count of four, and hold the exhale for a count of four. Repeat four times. Or
    b. Breathe in and out to a count of three, or in to a count of three and out to a count of six. When your exhale is longer than your inhale, you calm the

---

[13] See: https://www.heartmath.org/resources/heartmath-tools/

sympathetic nervous system—the flight, fright, or freeze part of you.
2. Get out in nature for a walk, if possible.
3. Reach out to a buddy or therapist—get the help you need.
4. This is the one- and five-minute technique. Ask yourself, what can I do or what needs to be done in the next minute? That's all you need to worry about—the very next minute. You can take all the other stuff off your shoulders; there is no need to carry those burdens right now. Move to the next five minutes when you are ready. What needs to be done in the next five minutes? You can increase the time to thirty minutes and so on if that resonates.
5. Sometimes you just must do something else, like binge-watch a show, space out, or be taken out to dinner by friends. When you just do something else "not to deal with it," you are safely processing your grief and loss, and this works. Come back to the situation when you can—planning the funeral, getting his stuff out of the house, job hunting, and so on.
6. Do something or everything on your self-soothe list. Do it—do many things on it—a lot.

Exercise 22—Create Your Self-Soothe List

This concept is juxtaposed to the idea of self-medicating, which is doing something—even a healthy thing—to excess. I used to have my soldiers make these and suggested they enjoy something on the list daily.

1. Get comfortable and write down all the things you enjoy doing that are reasonable, decent, and healthy for you to do. Again, we are not talking about playing video games all day or drinking more than is healthy. Make a list of the good

stuff and choose some things that can take five minutes, like making a cup of tea, and things that can take three minutes, a few hours, or all day. Some days you can't get away fishing, so what can you do in an hour? Be flexible with the time required for your various things.
2. Now do the things on the list quite often—daily. Not to self-medicating excess, of course, but often. Get used to thinking about this list and doing those things.
3. When you are freaking out a tad less and are emotionally able, do the things on your list as often as you can.

13

SOME GREAT AFFIRMATIONS

My life gets more fabulous every day.
~Louise Hay

Affirmations are great tools to change your subconscious and to get and experience what you want in life. You may have heard about them. Here are some guidelines for their use.

Bright and Positive

Keep your word choices positive. Instead of saying, "I'll be out of debt by Christmas," say, "I am financially free." Instead of "This medical diagnosis of ___ will be healed soon," say, "My body is healthy, fit, and strong. All my body functions are working perfectly." Say "I desire" instead of "I want." I would not write out or say an exact medical diagnosis; you may bring it more into reality. I choose words like "challenge" or "project."

There can be exceptions to using only bright and positive words. Many authors and students have successfully used seemingly negative words to great effect, and these cause no harm. Here you can use your own discernment.

"I now overcome negative beliefs."

"I no longer feel the need to criticize others."

Affirmations such as these, used sparingly, can be quite useful.

Ways to Use Affirmations

Affirmations are fun. You can write them down. Don't type them; it's more magical when you write. This is spell work, and using your body and handwriting is more effective. You can type out a list for reference, but I'd write them down by hand daily. You can write them out once or seven or ten times daily. Some enjoy the fifty-five times over five days plan. Others like the Tesla three, six, nine pattern. To use this, you plan out your mindset work in this pattern. For example, you can say them six times in a mirror, write them nine times, and repeat this three times each day. You can play with that.

You can speak them out loud in front of a mirror or while you are sitting with coffee or meditating. You can record them and listen to them, especially in the morning and evening when you are groggy. You can write them and place them near or under a candle, which you light. (Be safe.) You can use mala beads (or any type of beads) and recite them 108 or so times daily.

Don't Be Desperate

Wanting or desperate words tell your subconscious that you really want the thing, not that you have it, and will create circumstances in which you are still wanting it.

"I have to have her, or I will die. I want her so bad." Nope. You might say, "Lucy and I have the most beautiful romantic relationship. We love each other deeply. We harmonize wonderfully together."

Time Lag

There can be a time lag in getting what you want . . . and thank goodness for that. Otherwise, we'd all be in the hospital because of the anger, justified or not, of other drivers on the road. Neville Goddard says that anything you'd like to have immediately goes into your energy field and waits for you, meaning that creation is finished. It waits until you are ready to receive it: in other words, when you vibrate at having it. Some things take time; others are immediate. You also must watch how hard you think a thing will be to manifest, as this can make it take longer. Imagine everything is as easy as getting a free cup of coffee.

The Date Is Not Important

While it is good to give the subconscious a date by which you want the manifestation, it is not important. Do not worry about the date but have one. You don't have to have one for every affirmation, of course, but you may want to set a date for a very big goal.

Be Present

Write your affirmations in the present. Say "I am in a great romantic relationship" instead of "Someday I want to be in a great romantic relationship."

Leave Room for Something Better

We may not know what is best for us, and perhaps the universe has something way better. Have you ever looked back at a guy or gal you used to want? Aren't you relieved you did not get together? Or consider the job that didn't come through.

"All this or something better." I use this statement after my affirmation work to be sure I'm covered; this way, I receive every good thing.

Using Key Words

Another way to employ affirmations is to use two key words. You can simply recite "wealth, success" to yourself over and over when you think of it. You can fall asleep saying "wealth, success" (or "love, joy"—whatever).

Askformations

These are also fun. You ask yourself a question as an affirmation, and this gets your subconscious plotting how to get your goal. "How is it that I am a millionaire?" "Why am I so handsome?" "Why does he love me so much?" "How do I win every fitness contest?" "How am I so amazing and wonderful?" Your subconscious says, "Yeah, how *is* she a millionaire? We'd better figure this out. Oh, here's how!" And you get an idea for some inspired action.

"I Am" Statements

These are important. I ask my clients to write out twenty "I am" statements daily. They can be the same or different each day.

I am amazing and wonderful.
I am calm, serene, and poised.
I am happy, healthy, and wealthy.
I am healthy, strong, and fit.
I am the luckiest person.
I am bold, confident, adventurous, and courageous.
I am fun. I am funny.
I am psychic and intuitive.
I am getting better every day.
I am kind and loving.
I am a great writer, speaker, fisherman, vocalist, etc.
I am beautiful.
I am brilliant.
I am wealthy beyond measure.
I am always safe and protected.
I am financially free.
I prosper in all ways.
I am one with the infinite riches of my subconscious mind.
I am the best partner, mother, brother, coach, teacher, etc.
I am at my perfect weight.

Using Anthony Norvell's Key Word Program Method

This technique comes from Norvell's *Universal Secrets of Telecosmic Power*. It is related to the "I am" statements above. You choose ideal key words, such as "I unite" or "I receive," and craft an affirmation to follow it:

I unite: "I now unite with universal mind for all riches and abundance."

On the first day, you read the whole thing seven times. During the day, when you think about it, you recite "I unite" since the whole line is now programmed into your subconscious mind. For the next week or so, read the whole thing two or three times, both morning and night. The rest of the day, recite "I unite." After that, read it once in the morning and once at night while reciting "I unite" throughout the day as you see fit. Norvell suggests reciting "I unite" at least seven times during the day. Continue until you see the results. How easy is that? This is quite effective.

Here are some examples of words you can use:

> I unite
> I create
> I receive
> I progress
> I advance
> I earn
> I desire
> I release
> I achieve
> I create
> I declare
> I conquer
> I adjust
> I transmute
> I dissolve
> I love
> I increase
> I win
> I agree
> I enjoy
> I harmonize
> I change
> I multiply
> I replenish
> I subdue

I dominate
I project
I program
I overcome
I banish
I elevate
I recall
I evolve
I console
I remove
I attract
I refine
I illumine
I move
I control
I grow
I accumulate
I magnetize
I discover

Being Grateful

Another type of affirmation is a grateful statement. I tell my clients to write out five things they are happy and grateful for every morning. You can change these daily if you like.

"I am extremely happy and grateful that . . ."

And then I have them write out another five grateful statements, but this time for things they want to manifest, and they write them in the present tense.

Some Great Affirmations

Enjoy these. Modify them for your own use. You can read this list daily and feel the change in your life.

By day and by night, I prosper in all my interests.
Sales of my services are improving every day.
I prosper in all ways.
I am advancing, progressing, and getting wealthier every day.
I like money. I love it.
Everything I touch turns to gold.
I am successful in all I do.
I use money wisely, conscientiously, and judiciously.
Money is constantly circulating in my life.
I release money with joy, and it returns to me multiplied in a wonderful way.
Money is good, very good.
Money flows to me in avalanches of abundance.
I am a money magnet. Money loves me.
I use money for good, and I am grateful for my good and the riches of my mind.
Infinite intelligence governs and watches over all my financial transactions.
I manage my money beautifully.
Whatever I do prospers.
I am one with the infinite riches of my subconscious mind.
It is my right to be rich, happy, and successful.
Money flows to me freely, endlessly, and joyfully.
Large sums of money flow to me in increasing amounts through multiple sources on a continual basis.
I am forever conscious of my true worth.
I give of my talents freely, and I am wonderfully blessed financially.
I am financially free. It is wonderful.
I desire the sum of _____ for my financial freedom.

I desire the perfect home with wonderful furnishings.
I am the luckiest woman/man.
Reality is rigged in my favor.
Everything always works out for me.
Everything good always happens to me.
I improve by quantum leaps every day.
Wonderful things are always happening in my life.
I always have the best day ever.
I live in flow in a continual state of ecstasy and bliss.
I am always safe and protected.
I always receive money in many ways.
I have money without needing to work for it or earn it.
Money just comes to me.
It's so easy and fun to receive money.
Money sticks to me.
I am highly favored by money.
Money is always looking for me, seeking me out, finding me, and coming to me.

I easily and joyously receive money.

I watch money flow into my bank accounts every single day—all the time.

Every day I receive deposits into my bank accounts.

I receive all different amounts of money, usually very large amounts.

I am worthy of the riches that flow to me in an unending and unlimited supply.

I increase my money supply from my present limitations to an unlimited flow that comes to me from many channels.

I believe I am worthy of the best of everything, and I now increase my expectations to include the best the world has to offer.

I increase my money awareness from small sums to large sums.

I project the mental images of money to the infinite intelligence that created all things and ask that my life be blessed with riches and comfort.

I claim riches and abundance as my natural heritage, for I know God created the universe and all therein for me to use and enjoy.

I receive from the universe the sum of ___ so I may pay my bills now. I receive more money in my work or from unexpected sources in increasing amounts for my financial freedom.

I am eager to progress in my work, to win a promotion, and to enjoy more pay.

I do work in which I am independent, earning more than ___ each year for work that is pleasant for me.

I desire the sum of ___ for immediate expenses and the larger sums of ___ and ___ for travel and other fun. I also program the sum of ___ for future financial security.

My flow of money now obeys the impulses of my subconscious mind and begins to come to me from unexpected as well as expected sources.

There is enormous wealth in the universe, and I now claim my share of money, goods, houses, land, and possessions of every kind.

Money, or its equivalent, now flows into my pockets and bank accounts.

I am blessed with abundant riches to meet my every need and desire.

I have good luck in contests for money. I always win. I am in a winning cycle.

Every day, in every way, I am getting better and better.

I am happy, healthy, and wealthy.

I am fit, healthy, and strong.

My body gets more fit every day.

All my body functions are working beautifully.

I do great yoga. I am a fabulous runner. I do excellent CrossFit.

I win at everything I do.

I am growing younger and younger daily.

I increase my gifts and talents through study and development of all my potential.

I know I was born to success, and I now increase my powers of concentration and projection so I can impress everyone who can help me achieve my goals.

I see myself as the center of a world that is richly endowed with every type of treasure and every fun thing.

I see myself having the money to travel in luxury all over the world.

I see myself meeting important and interesting people who enjoy my company and enrich my life.

I see myself living an amazing life with my romantic partner/spouse. We love each other deeply, live in a beautiful home together, and travel the world.

I claim all the things I desire, here and now.

I am living a life that is better than my dreams.

My conscious mind now unites perfectly with the subconscious and superconscious minds that perform miracles for me.

I unite my mind with the intelligent infinity that rules the universe.

I now ask for immediate guidance.

I have the right work, the right income, the perfect love (marriage, family), and larger sums of money for financial freedom and security.

I now have my problems/challenges solved, and I now create my perfect life.

Unity prevails in my life, and there is no confusion. I have harmony in my home, my work, and my surroundings.

I ask that my interests be advanced. I ask that I move to the highest income level and the highest recognition and fame.

I wish to move into a new area of work that earns more than ____ each year. This work involves fun travel and offers me fame and recognition in my field of choice.

I desire peace of mind and soul.

I now attract my right work, which I enjoy, and I am a huge success in my work.

I am now enjoying the awareness that I am working toward my life's higher goals.

I am no longer content with an ordinary life. I now achieve the greatest, create the most beautiful, and aspire to the attainment of my highest goals.

I am now inspired by lofty ideals that have motivated geniuses of the past. I duplicate their deeds. I emulate their patterns of thought.

I now have fame and success. I have recognition, money, and other rewards from life. I am popular, and I have the respect of my friends and family.

I now own my own business.

I do something creative and outstanding.

I live in a beautiful home that is comfortably furnished.

I instruct my higher mind to program a career for me in which I am a famous at _____.

I now create and project to my conscious mind the desire to create high and inspiring ideas to project through my voice, my personality, and my thoughts.

I now charm and enchant people through my magnetism.

I now sway public opinion through my thoughts and ideals.

I desire to entertain, instruct, inspire, uplift, heal, and encourage millions of people through my own creative work.

I project rhythm, motion, and grace in my body, my voice, and my presence in patterns of light and beauty—bringing relaxation, enjoyment, healing, and inspiration to audiences all over the world.

I choose social media, news programs, the public stage, TV, and movies to project my talents for public acclaim.

I emulate the highest standards in my field, and I perfect myself so I am worthy of the rich rewards commensurate with my talents and efforts.

I now express my creative talents in business and industry and achieve the highest goal possible.

I receive brilliant, million-dollar ideas in my field.

I act on these wonderful ideas, which are converted to money, fame, glory, and success.

My subconscious mind now releases to me golden streams of fantastic ideas, inventions, business methods, secret formulas, skills, and other elements I require so I reach the highest pinnacle of success.

I have peace in my mind and in my environment.

I manage to avoid the misfortunes and challenges of the outer world.

I withdraw within my citadel of spirit and strength and conquer my mind, my tongue, and my temper.

All obstacles and obstructions are now instantly removed, and I am the center of peace and calm.

No outer force has the power to disturb my serenity, peace, calm, and poise.

I remove friction.

I remove opposition.

I remove discord and anger and dwell in inner stillness.

All my challenges are instantly dissolved in light and justice.

All persons, conditions, situations, and objects in my world are subject to a law that is higher than the material and the physical.

I invoke that law in this moment.

I conquer my temper and my tongue.

I conquer time and space.

I remove all obstructions and impediments and see only a perfect flow of the stream of consciousness removing every negative force from my mind, body, soul, and environment.

I now adjust to that which I cannot change; I am now in harmony with all people; and I direct love, understanding, and forgiveness to them. I adjust to change.

I adjust to discord by holding thoughts of harmony within myself.

I now transmute all negative forces to energies for my highest and best good.

I now dissolve all challenges that affect my life. They are here and now dissolved in the light of truth.

I know the means are at hand to overcome all negative challenges in my work, relationships, etc.

My partner and I are united in bonds of love, and no external force can intrude in our lives.

All my challenges are now dissolving.

My partner (person, child, etc.) and I are bound together in mutual trust, love, and respect.

My mind is now released from all sense of possessiveness. Love must be freely given and freely taken, and I cannot hold what is not mine. I now release my partner, having full trust that they want to share every wonderful experience with me fully.

I recognize the need to give credit where it is deserved, and I easily praise others.

I release the need to criticize others.

I only offer advice if I am asked to give it.

My partner and I are united in bonds of love, and our union is blessed by God. Together, we overcome all challenges.

I know that love requires mutual respect, tolerance, and a sense of freedom.

I agree with all that is good, honorable, and honest.

I now program harmony and unity in my environment.

I radiate an aura of confidence, poise, peace, and power.

I am agreeable, pleasant, and friendly, and others react in a like manner.

I dare to be different. The great things others have done, I can do, too.

I dare to meet the daily challenges of life knowing that I can overcome them.

I dare to develop my hidden potential for greatness.

I dare to overcome the discouraging remarks of my family and friends.

I dare to dream and think big, knowing that nothing is impossible for me to achieve.

I now have a million-dollar destiny.

I believe in myself and my destiny.

I believe I am worthy of a great destiny.

I now build my new self-image of charm, magnetism, and radiance.

I am now successful in my work.

I desire the best that life has to offer.

I have a fortune, so I may have all the things I desire.

Everyone I meet responds to me with friendliness and helps me achieve my goals.

I can be anything in life I choose to be.

I overcome all my negative emotions, and I radiate a cheerful, optimistic, and hopeful quality that attracts others.

ID# 14

MY DAILY THINGS

> A champion doesn't become a champion in the ring; he's merely recognized in the ring. His "becoming" happens during his daily routine.
>
> ~Joe Louis

I offer this humbly for your perusal. I am a work in progress. I do change things up now and then, such as my fasting routine; sometimes it's three days a month, five days a month, one day a week, or a seven-day fast once a year. Right now, I fast the first five business days of every month so as not to ruin a weekend. Every item I mention here is a study unto itself; each thing I do daily is a result of at least six months of study and research.

Most of our current habits are built into us as belief systems; we have emotional attachments to what we do and don't do, and we make up psychological reasons for them. My daughter said to me the other day, "Oh, I could never fast; I get too hangry."

Yes, because her human microbiome of yeast, bacteria, and protozoans punishes her for not keeping her blood sugar level up to feed them. She could push past that with twenty-four hours of an uncomfortable fast. She is habitually and culturally used to eating a Snickers bar at three p.m., and she is ordered to eat it by her personal microbiome with hormonal rewards and punishment. You can beat your microbiome, but change is hard.

Let's look at my current schedule, which is always subject to change.

I rise at six a.m.

As I lie in bed, I think of five things I am extremely happy and grateful for and why, and say them to myself:

"I am extremely happy and grateful that my home is clean, organized, and repaired. I love living in a gorgeous, well-maintained home, and I enjoy having people over."

Then I think and say to myself five things I am grateful for that haven't happened yet. I state these in the present tense:

"I am extremely happy and grateful for my five-hundred-hour yoga teacher training certificate from Yoga Alliance. I like that I can add this body of knowledge to my coaching."

Then I look at myself in the mirror for thirty to sixty seconds, and I say really nice things:

"Hi! Look at me, so beautiful. I am amazing. I have so much talent and abundance, and I am great at helping others. My business is booming. I always have the best day ever. Wonderful things are always happening in my life."

I gently scrape my tongue with a copper tongue scraper ten times, back to front. This is Ayurvedic medicine, and it's important to clean the tongue to wake up the digestive process. Tongue scraping supports a clean mouth—this helps the breath.

I brush with fluoride-free toothpaste, rinse, then floss—you'd be amazed how much less is between your teeth after you brush. I use fluoride-free mouthwash afterward.

Then I place half a teaspoon or so of coconut oil in my mouth and swish for five minutes while I'm doing other chores. This is oil pulling—coconut oil clears bacteria and prevents them from entering the bloodstream; it clears plaque from the teeth and whitens them over time. You can also use sesame oil. Do not spit the coconut oil in the sink; it may clog.

Again, I look at myself in the mirror and state my big goal for five minutes to myself. For example:

"I am so happy and grateful I earn ___ every month, and I love it. I do what I love and love what I do, serving at the highest level."

Most mornings, before I shower, I dry-brush my skin. I tend to do this in the shower stall before I turn on the water. This gets the lymphatic system flowing and cleans the skin. A few times each month, I will clean each nasal sinus with a neti pot. Be sure to lean way down in the sink when you use a neti pot in each nostril to be sure no liquid goes down your throat. You just want to have it flow out of your other nostril. This is not a pleasant experience, but it's good to clean out your sinus and nasal area. This is all part of Ayurvedic medicine.

I make matcha tea and drink it while I meditate. Yes, I meditate with a hot beverage; it's delightful. I will either do guided imagery with myself, imagine mental movies for my goals, or pay attention to my breath while posing questions to Source:

"How do I solve this problem? How is it that I might . . .?" And I wait for an answer, either in word, thought, or picture. Sometimes I will empower my biofield and place all my virtues and qualities and desires into it, as if I am bringing to myself all I desire to have and to be. There are a thousand different ways to meditate.

I will do some yoga, like forty minutes of power yoga, Bikram (twenty-six plus two hot yoga), Ashtanga, or the five Tibetans. The five Tibetan exercises only take five to ten minutes and are magical—and/or I will do a high-intensity interval training (HIIT)-style workout, a run, or a ruck march.

I will make another warm beverage.

I write out my main goal ten times and my life script, which is ten to fifteen sentences describing my big goal. I write out twenty "I am" statements: "I am brilliant," "I am abundant and prosperous," and so on.

I do various chores around the house or yard, pay a bill or two, or do other office work. I take about thirty minutes to do the immediate daily have-tos for the day.

I aim to get to my client work and three to six goal-achieving activities for the day between nine and ten a.m. You want to plan backward from when you need to begin your workday and leave at least two hours for all your morning "you" time.

I aim not to eat until two p.m. and tend to eat one or two meals, with my eating window ending around seven p.m. This is flexible. Sometimes I choose one meal a day (OMAD). I eat cleanly as I currently see it. I allow myself to fill a bowl or plate for each meal. These days, I'm fasting the first five business days each month, with only a twelve-ounce cup of matcha tea in the morning for my soul and some electrolytes. I save dry fasts for other times when I can take a retreat with myself.

Now, eating, oh boy. I can hear the complaining now. People will say, "Oh, I can't wait to eat that long; I get hangry." "Oh, I couldn't fast." Oh my goodness, I used to think the same thing. We often give in to our habits, culture, and emotional comfiness. One can develop this ability. I have fasted since my teens and did hard, soul-wrenching work to fast back then. It was a huge trial to work on my emotional need to eat. And you can be a pro at it, even if you struggle with eating issues as I did. No judgment—you do you.

And you can flex. Tonight, I'm meeting some girlfriends at our favorite bar and restaurant. I will eat and drink past seven. Everything in moderation, including moderation. I fast and intermittently fast so I can cover my fun eating and for body health.

I do my work throughout the day. I aim to improve 1 percent every day in one or more things—be it working with clients better, learning more coaching skills, organizing a drawer, being better online with Zoom, trimming trees in the yard, or painting wall trim. I aim to take care of my body, health, cars, yard, home, friends, family, grandkids, and so on a little each day. I aim to do the next right thing the right way. It doesn't *all* get done, but some of it does.

In the evening, I take time to ponder the following:

1. What were my wins?
2. Did I improve 1 percent in some way?
3. Did I leave the woodpile higher than I found it?
4. Did I take extreme responsibility for myself?
5. Did I say a hard no to things that don't support my goals—be they requests, events, or silly people?
6. What could I do better? Can I repair a relationship? Make a call?
7. What three to six goal activities can I tackle tomorrow?

I might do more yoga or the five Tibetan exercises.

In the evening, I'll do something fun with family, friends, or my person: watch a movie, play a game, laugh, and have fun. I make fun plans for the weekend for a moment or for a day or two.

I ponder the three to six activities in the evening so my subconscious can be working on them while I sleep, seeking the best way to do them or shorten the time or expense they'll take. Life is much easier when you employ your subconscious. Relying only on your conscious/logical mind might keep you tied up or stuck.

Not medical advice: I usually do not take Western meds. I use naturopathic stuff I research, like essential oils, herbs, meditation, yoga, and Ayurveda. I do my best to reach wellness and well-being on my own. You may need to go the allopathic route. When I mentioned that each thing I do is the result of at least six months of study, I meant it.

How to Begin

Try one thing you are curious about. Maybe get a tongue scraper online. Research it; try it out for a month. See what you think. And, as you are able, make another change the next month. Your research will lead you to wonderful things. A friend just told me about the five Tibetan exercises recently, and they have changed my life. There is always more to learn and do. We didn't get stuck in a day, and we won't fix it all in a day. You may spend many months researching various eating styles or mindset techniques, for example. Perhaps for you, fitness is a good one-mile walk, not yoga. Or you choose to record and listen to your "I am" and goal statements, not write them out. Great!

Try one new thing a month while you do your research. Maybe doing one meal a day (OMAD) is scary right now. You can start intermittent fasting with a window from ten a.m. to seven p.m. to start and close the window over time. For many years, I just ate three modest bowls of food each day. That worked, too. You can investigate various diet regimens for yourself; this is not medical or nutritional advice.

This is not a rigid list; I am not necessarily right, and I don't necessarily have the best way. This is *a* way to live. I have also enjoyed many months of blowout when I did very little on this list. I will always have some regimen for myself, even if it changes somewhat from what I've described here.

In any case, if you'd like some assistance or have any questions, feel free to reach out. I am not overly attached to my things. I do these great daily habits, so I don't always have to do them. I may go on vacation and forget the coconut oil.

www.ingramcontent.com/pod-product-compliance
Lightning Source LLC
Chambersburg PA
CBHW072211070526
44585CB00015B/1288